MW01259117

The Art of
COOKING
OMELETTES

THE ART OF

Cooking Omelettes

Madame Romaine de Lyon

ECHO POINT BOOKS & MEDIA, LLC

Published by Echo Point Books & Media
www.EchoPointBooks.com

ISBN: 978-1-62654-950-0

Cover photography by Karl Hutchinson:
Flickr.com/photos/whateverthing
Contact:
KARL HUTCHINSON PHOTOGRAPHY
KarHutPhoto@gmail.com

Cover design by Adrienne Nunez,
Echo Point Books & Media

Printed in the U. S. A.

Contents

INTRODUCTION

CHAPTER ONE
How I Came to Be an Omelette Maker   9

CHAPTER TWO
How to Cook an Omelette   39

CHAPTER THREE
Omelette Recipes   51

CHAPTER FOUR
The Salad   140

CHAPTER FIVE
Wine with Omelettes — and without   144

CHAPTER SIX
Some Notes on Omelette Eaters   148

INDEX   157

Recipes shown in the text in small capital letters may be found by consulting the Index.

✤ INTRODUCTION

In 1920, Madame Romaine de Lyon found herself alone in New York City. Her husband Joannes suddenly and unexpectedly passed away from a heart attack, leaving Romaine, barely able to speak English and with few cultural or social ties, to find her own way. Drawing upon the household and management skills that she later attributed to the traditionally French parenting style of her mother, Romaine forged ahead with her new life in America. She opened a small *salon de thé*, a casual tea house that also serves meals.

Through subtle twists of fate, Romaine's salon slowly transformed first into a simple omelette restaurant, then into an iconic New Your City institution. For 65 years, Mme Romaine maintained a midtown presence, where the anonymous and celebrity alike savored over 500 variations of omelettes available from her extraordinary menu. The screenplay for *The Producers* was penned by Mel Brooks at his regular table in the back of the restaurant. Anne Bancroft, Joan Rivers, Mary Tyler Moore, Joan Rivers, and many other celebrities were known to stop in for omelettes as well.

Romaine's dedication to the proper execution of the omelette and her reputation as expert of her craft spread beyond the limits of New York City. Her stature as a master omelette maker was evidenced by signed photos that covered the restaurant walls from famous customers who lived all over the world. Her small restaurant was also chosen to premier Teflon-coated pans to the American public. But perhaps the best recognition of all came from the ultimate cooking authority, the great Julia Child. During the omelette episode of *The French Chef*, Julia holds up a copy of *The Art of Cooking Omelettes* and recommends it to anyone interested in cooking exquisite omelettes. To the discerning, anything less is simply not an *œuf!*

The Art of Cooking Omelettes captures the heart and essence of Romaine's storied life. The content and her lively writer's voice offer insight into Romaine's personal history and philosophy of life (culinary and otherwise). This autobiography of a master omelette maker could stand alone as a worthy read, but *The Art of Cooking Omelettes* also includes recipes for over 500 of the omelettes, culinary works of art that made Madame Romaine de Lyon's restaurant so beloved. In lieu of the family life that fate took away from Mme Romaine, she dedicated herself to her customers, her craft, and her eggs. To our benefit, she has shared this passion with us in this delightful book.

—*André Boisseau*

❧ ❧ ❧   CHAPTER 1

How I Came to Be an Omelette Maker

No one comes into this world an instinctive maker of omelettes, and I would not have you believe that as soon as I could walk I toddled into the kitchen, seized an egg and a frying pan, and began at once what was to be my life's work. But I did have the inestimable advantage of being born in Lyon, France, where my parents maintained a restaurant in the tradition of true Lyonnaise cookery. As a young girl I was apprenticed to my mother in this family enterprise. She was an instinctive *cuisinière*, and saw to it that I learned in proper order: first, principles; then recipes; and, finally, style.

She taught me well. My omelettes have made me known in New Delhi and Hongkong, in Buenos Aires and Rio de Janeiro, in London and Paris, and everywhere in the United States. The people I have cooked for who came from these and other places all over the world have often said to me, "Oh, madame, will I be able to learn to make an omelette like yours?" This book is my answer. As my mother taught me, I will teach you the principles. To these you must add more than a soupçon of patience. I will give you, too, the recipes I have spent a lifetime perfecting. To these you must add practice.

When you have come that far, you will realize something else—that omelettes are also made with love and delicacy. These ingredients are not to be measured by the teaspoonful, but the good cook must bring them eventually to her pan and her eggs. The superior omelette is far more than breaking the eggs into the pan and applying heat. One begins with principles and practice, as I have said; the love and delicacy come naturally, if they are to come at all.

I will tell you how I became an omelette maker—not that you must emulate me to be successful, but perhaps you will want to know how one becomes Queen of the Omelette Makers, as they sometimes call me. It has been, believe me, a very long and sometimes a very rough road.

When I was only twelve and growing up in Lyon, I was traveling that road without knowing it. In those long days I went to school from eight o'clock until noon, and then from two o'clock until six. Most of my friends had time for play after supper, but I had to run straight home from school to help in the family restaurant. It was in a section called Monplaisir la Plaine, about as far from the center of Lyon as Times Square is from East 56th Street, where I have my restaurant between Park and Lexington avenues.

While I set out piles of dishes, peeled vegetables, and tended the soup, I could hear the shouts of my friends at play, but I did not think myself badly used, an unpaid convenience or drudge. My mother was a good French mother, who believed that her daughter must learn to become a proper manager, an art which no French girl is ever too young to begin learning. It was made clear to me that my mother was training me in that art, day by day. In the end I would be an excellent housekeeper, laundress, and seamstress, and naturally an excellent cook.

My parents, Pierre and Marie Chatard, were not born Lyonnais. They came from the Department of the Loire, but since the French believe that newly married couples should be left to work out their own affairs, they at once put a distance between themselves and their parental homes and came to Lyon. It is not considered a good thing for a French bride to be always running back to mother for advice and help, and that is why girls are given an early and thorough training in the tasks and responsibilities of keeping a home. That was the way my mother had been trained; it was the way she was training me when I was only twelve.

My father had been a horticulturist in the beginning, but had been compelled to give it up because of a fever and old war wounds, the result of his military service in Algeria. The fever affected him especially in the spring, when a horticulturist had the most work to do, so he concluded that he must change occupations and became the proprietor of a restaurant.

By chance he was soon able to increase his opportunities. An elderly couple named Caffer lived on a large estate adjoining his Restaurant de la Place and became regular patrons. They were so pleased with his menu and his management that they were soon friends as well, and suggested one day that he build a larger establishment, which they would be happy to finance.

It was done. The handsome new restaurant was located directly on the Place des Ecoles, a large square, and its sidewalk café section ran for nearly a full block. In addition to the main restaurant space, there was a room of tremendous proportions which provided accommodations for banquets, wedding dinners and suppers, political gatherings, and other local meetings.

My father, who was a shrewd man, saw that this room would be even more profitable as a civic meeting place if the streetcar line from the center of Lyon could only be extended as far as our square. He got up a petition to that effect, and when he had obtained enough signatures, took it to Monsieur Edouard Herriot, then mayor of the city. Monsieur Herriot received it favorably, the line was extended, and that was why the name of our restaurant was changed to Restaurant Terminus. On the day the first streetcar rattled into the Place des Ecoles, the end of the line, my father was host at a civic banquet in his big room. Monsieur Herriot came and made a little speech in which he expressed his satisfaction that the people of Monplaisir would no longer be obliged to walk two kilometers to the car line.

After that day, the mayor came often to our restaurant, sometimes officially in connection with public events, but more often privately with his friends. He enjoyed my mother's cuisine. His special delight was a chicken dish listed on the menu as *poulet Marie*, which she made in a wonderful sauce with truffles, mushrooms, and cognac. Often, as I looked up from taking something out of the oven, I would observe Monsieur Herriot eating slowly, savoring his chicken. If he happened to glance into the kitchen and caught my mother's eye, he would nod approvingly.

Mother began to train me early in soups and the simpler sauces. I thought of her as a pleasant woman but never a laughing one, and I admired her petite brunette good looks. She instructed me as much by quietly expert example as by spoken words. If I longed sometimes to be free to go out and play with my friends, there was compensation in the overwhelming pride I felt when patrons came out into the kitchen to look around. They looked about approvingly at the complete, shining order of the place, with the ranks of copper pans and kettles gleaming from the polishing with salt and vinegar I had given them. "What a kitchen!" these patrons would sigh, no doubt thinking of their own.

I worked hard to achieve the high standards my mother set, although I must confess that at the moment my ambitions were far from the kitchen. Secretly, I wanted to be a milliner or a *couturière* when I grew up. I would not have believed that one day I would have a restaurant of my own three thousand miles away in New York City.

One day, when I was just past thirteen, my mother startled me by announcing matter-of-factly, "Romaine, there is a party of young men about to leave for their military service and they have engaged a table for their going-away banquet. You will prepare the menu for them."

Such a responsibility suddenly thrust upon me! I was in a panic. I knew enough of such affairs to understand that they must be at once practical and sentimental—that is, the boys would have only a little money to spend, but because it was such a special occasion the meal must be planned so that it would appear as expensive as though it had been cooked for a gourmet.

With much changing of the mind and a growing nervousness, I made up my menu. I would begin, I thought, with assorted hors d'oeuvre, followed by *quenelles de brochet* with a tomato sauce. The main dish would be *tournedos au Madère*, I decided, and of course a salad, petits fours, and cheese. To this list I made a prophetic addition: *omelette au rhum*, for dessert.

Knowing that my mother would not be tolerant of failure, I swallowed my self-doubts and plunged in. To my pleasant surprise, things went well. I remembered every detail, even the flowers for the table. When the guests came I heard one of the young men worrying that the officials might reject him, but as the meal began and I noticed his large size and appetite to match, I surprised myself by my own temerity, remarking to him, "If they don't accept you, monsieur, I think they will not accept anybody." That made him laugh and he seemed to feel better.

So went my debut in cuisine. When the young men departed they gave me a nice tip, mother gave me one of her rare approving smiles, and I was satisfied.

It is easy to see how a restaurant could become a family affair, as ours was, although of my two brothers, one died at seventeen and the other was never interested in the restaurant. But our establishment was not only a family affair, as so many are in France, it was also quite in keeping with the national tradition that a restaurant is not a place where parents go to get away from the children. The family goes as a family, and the children learn to appreciate the joys of good food at an early age.

Our restaurant was a pleasant place to comtemplate on Sunday. The part fronting on the street contained not only the large dining room but a place for billiard tables. At the rear the kitchen opened out on gardens which my father had landscaped so that the patrons might sit and admire the trees and flowers. If they liked, they could also admire the fruits and berries he was growing for their enjoyment in the non-landscaped parts. If they ordered strawberries during the season, they had the satisfaction of knowing that they had been picked within the hour.

The flower gardens were not entirely ornamental. They supplied decoration for the tables, and it was my father's pleasure to give his women patrons little bouquets or nose-gays. Deftly and carefully he planted his gardens so that no matter how many blooms were picked, the plots would never appear thinned out.

Beside the gardens were ten *jeux de boules* (outdoor bowling alleys), an inevitable fixture in Lyon. No one can be considered really a Lyonnais if he does not follow this sport. Both professionals and amateurs play. There is always a tournament somewhere in the city on Sunday, with prizes. Such prizes! One is pleased to get one of the first few prizes, which are money, but it is no less a pleasure to be awarded the last prize, which is always a *saucisson de Lyon*, the classic sausage of the region. *Magnifique!*

On Sunday, therefore, our patrons came to bowl and play billiards as well as to eat. For the children, father put up a swing in a shady place, and on occasion when there was a quiet moment in the kitchen, I had my turn at swinging. Gardens and bowling grounds alike were enclosed with a system of *tonnelles*, rose and grape arbors, arranged so that groups could be served out of doors in fine weather. If they wished, patrons were free to help themselves to a rose or two, or a ripe bunch of grapes.

In the very large room used for public events, weddings and banquets, there were other entertainments all year long. In winter there were balls once a month, and performances of the Guignol Lyonnais, long associated with the city and second only to the Grand Guignol of Paris. Then there were marionette shows, in which the puppets enacted tales about Lyon, little operas, and clever parodies peculiarly Lyonnaise.

We could seat four hundred people about a horseshoe table in this big room. On such grand occasions, we had to hire an extra woman to help clean and peel the vegetables, as well as extra waiters. No outsider was permitted to cook, however. Mother did it all, as usual, with me as her trained helper. It was at these banquets I first learned to cook a chicken so that in the broth I would have the elements for at least six different sauces. Since then I have learned many more ways to make sauce with chicken broth—Béchamel, sauce with sherry added; sauce with madeira, with cognac, with cream, with tomato. These are best started with chicken broth.

Unfortunately, because of the popularity of Lyonnaise potatoes, many people in this country think that onions are the secret of Lyonnaise cuisine. They are not. They are used and respected, but the real secret is the inspired use of what I would call honorable materials, used to the full for exactly what they are, never arranged with two meanings, but always with exquisite consideration for the whole.

Another reason for the excellence of Lyonnaise cuisine is the absence of indiscretions with herbs and spices. With us, the soupçon is esteemed. This is not only sound cooking but sound philosophy as well. In cookery, whether it be the simplest or the finest, there should be an element of mystery, even of intrigue. How much more artistic to present a dish which invites the imagination, a pleasant mood of "*Mon dieu, but that is good! What is it?*" rather than a dish in which a blast of flavoring abruptly ends all guessing.

But if we use herbs and spices with discretion, we do not hold back when wine is to be used in a dish. When I make my chicken in wine sauce, I use both wine and sherry, and I do not skimp on them.

Lyonnaise cooking, then, is the result of integrity and the sophisticated use of materials which are in no way themselves sophisticated. By integrity I mean the avoidance of such horrors as bottled extracts, butter substitutes, or prepared sauces. By sophistication I do not imply a high cost, by any means. The true Lyonnaise *cuisinière* prefers for texture and flavor many varieties of fish which have no claim to elegance. In the matter of wines, too, sophistication means often the deliberate use of everyday wines in preference to vintage. And always only the very best in cream, butter, and eggs.

For centuries Lyon did not know of any other butter but the sweet variety. Then, during the First World War, salt butter made an appearance in the city, to the mystification of the citizens, who called it "American butter." It met with no visible favor; its virtues were not understood. For myself, I would never think of using anything but sweet butter to make my omelettes and cook my meats, and I will tell you why. When you put salt butter in the pan, a little water emerges because of the salt. I do not care for that. My omelettes have no need for water in the pan.

I grew up with such principles under my mother's training, always aware of traditional pronouncements like the one attributed to La Mère Filloux, born Françoise Fayolle, who declared: "It takes years of study and experience to produce a perfect dish. I have spent my life perfecting five or six dishes. I will serve only these, and I will be sure of doing them perfectly." These were the standards my mother set me.

To one who aspires to become a specialist in one dish—the omelette, in this case—I recommend highly taking the trouble to learn something about the materials you will use. By the time I had assembled recipes for even half of the more than five hundred kinds of omelettes now on my menu, I was using in one combination or another all the ingredients I learned about as a child in Lyon. My mother not only taught me the principles of combining materials, but she transmitted to me her understanding of both the obvious and the more subtle distinctions in the materials themselves. "There is little or no prejudice in nature," I can hear her saying. "Nature, if you understand it and help it along a bit, produces harmonious combinations."

We were always very close to nature in Lyon, sometimes in ways that would be startling here in America today. I remember a Sunday when one of our patrons arrived in a worried state. He was a well-known sculptor who always drove to the restaurant in an equipage of charm, which would be called a pony cart in America—a trap, as it was known in the old days. The body was wicker, mounted on strong wheels of lightweight metal, with spokes that shone and twinkled. The animal that drew this equipage was a handsome little cob, short and stout, but invariably amiable.

On this day, however, the horse appeared as worried as its owner, who said to my father as he drew rein, "Monsieur Chatard, I think we have here some *maladie* which has descended suddenly. I am afraid it is colic, and I do not know how to proceed. I do not suppose that there is at this moment among your patrons a veterinarian?"

My father had a warm feeling for all domestic animals, especially for horses. He put the palm of his hand over the feverish muzzle of the little horse and spoke soothingly to it, running his hands gently over its quivering sides. "Do not agitate yourself, monsieur," he said to the sculptor. "I can do something."

A few patrons, arriving for their dinner, by this time had gathered and were watching the scene with lively interest. My father hurried indoors and came out again with a liquid in a water tumbler. He spoke again encouragingly to the animal, which was now groaning feebly. Tipping back its head, he poured the contents of the tumbler down the horse's throat. "There," he said confidently to the sculptor. "You will see, monsieur."

It was astonishing to see how quickly the quivering body

quieted. The little horse shook its head vigorously several times, and seemed before our eyes to regain its health and pleasant nature. There was a small approving cheer from the crowd, and the eyes of the sculptor opened wide.

"What was it?" he inquired respectfully.

"Absinthe," my father answered calmly. "It is the best treatment for colic in man or beast." It is true. To this day, if I have colic, a dose of absinthe rids me of it instantly.

The sculptor was so enchanted that he gave me a very nice present. His wife gave me a present too, believing the one given by her husband was not enough.

I might have lived on in Lyon in this charming atmosphere if life had not begun to take another turn for me, although I did not yet know it. Among our family friends were a couple, Monsieur and Madame Champion and their son Joannes, ten years old. Monsieur Champion was a well-known blender of perfumes. He died suddenly and Madame Champion decided to go to the United States to establish a future for herself and her son and daughter, but she did not want to take the boy to a strange country unless there were definite prospects of support. It was arranged, therefore, that he would stay in our house for a year until she sent for him. During that year Joannes and I became good companions, and I was most unhappy when the time ended and he went away to America. He was then eleven years old.

Soon after, I finished my school work and continued for a time to help in the kitchen and restaurant. But I longed to make my own way and thought more and more of becoming a *couturière*. I enrolled in L'Ecole Commerciale de la Martinière, and because my mother had given me such a good knowledge of sewing, I did well and was able before long to design and make my own clothes.

Meanwhile, like any girl, I was interested in boys. Working

in the restaurant made it quite simple for me to meet and know many young men. At the monthly balls in the large room I had a partner for every dance, and there was always a boy, often more than one, to sit with me at the performances of Le Guignol Lyonnais.

But French family custom was very strict. My parents absolutely forbade me to be alone with a young man away from the restaurant, not even for a walk in the park. That was not always easy to endure, but I had been brought up with an unquestioning respect for the family's honor, which I understood my father was doing his best to protect. It was not enough for a daughter to be virtuous in fact; she must also avoid any slightest appearance of being otherwise.

I was allowed to receive young men at home, but they had to be approved by my father, who took this duty with extreme seriousness. If he had any reason to disapprove a young man, he had a way of dismissing him with an embarrassing finality. I remember an evening when I was with my one true love—of that week—and was exhibiting, no doubt, even more than the usual signs of total involvement. My father appeared on the veranda, where we were dreaming over a vermouth cassis, and remarked coolly to my love, "Ah, monsieur, you appear to be leaving." The thought could not have been farther from the poor fellow's mind. While he was still getting to his feet in complete confusion, my father went on inexorably, "I must ask you not to call on my daughter again."

That time I was utterly devastated, and stormed and cried. How could my father be so insensible? How unlike him! We did not speak of it again, and avoided each other for a while. I never discovered what the reason for this abrupt dismissal might have been.

A short time after that incident, Madame Champion returned from the United States on a visit to Lyon. She entertained us for hours with tales of far-off America, especially how she had invested in a theatrical hotel, of which she was now the owner. She had me spellbound with her stories of people in the theater. As for Joannes, it did not seem possible to me that he was grown and on the point of opening a small silk factory in New York. That was a logical direction for his life to have taken, because the manufacture of silk is the chief industry of Lyon, and he had grown up with it.

I did not know it at the time, but Madame Champion was a matchmaker. When she returned to New York, she remarked casually to Joannes that he would naturally be thinking about marrying a French girl, and in fact, if he did not mind her saying so, she knew of one in particular, one whom he already knew, a girl who could cook and sew and do all the other things expected of a French bride.

Dismayed by what seemed to me to be endless parental objections to my would-be suitors, I was in a susceptible frame of mind when a letter arrived from Joannes Champion, asking me to marry him. Soon would be best, he wrote; in fact, to speak of his feelings, the sooner the better.

I was filled with the greatest excitement of my life. A new world opened before me.

"You are too young," my father said with finality.

"But—"

"New York is far away!" my mother cried, tears falling down her cheeks, "too far. We would never see you again. It is too much, with one of your brothers dead and Jean-Marie away doing his military service. We would be robbed of all our children, our comfort! We need you with us!"

Was it possible, I asked myself, that my family secretly cherished the hope of retaining for their old age the sustaining company of an unmarried daughter? It was possible; it happened every day in French families. *Quelle erreur!*

But if I could not agree with my family, at least I understood them. And to myself I admitted more than a little fear of leaving the familiar things I had known all my life and going so far away. I gave in to their objections, telling myself there was nothing else to do.

"Thank you for the honor," I wrote Joannes. "I am sorry to be unable to accept." Then I gave myself over to being miserable for a time.

It did not last. I was young and spirited, and there was much to take up my time. The first great war had ended, and our family was happy to have Jean-Marie returned to us in good health, although he had been a prisoner for four years. Ten thousand young men of Lyon had been killed, and many others maimed for life. The city itself was touched with a new prosperity and an accompanying gaiety. New fortunes were made, new buildings sprang up.

In the midst of it, our fortunes ran the other way. My father's health began to fail, and we had to sell our restaurant. He bought a small piece of property on the outskirts of Lyon where he could find rest and quiet, and there he was free to take up horticulture again if he chose. The change seemed to revive him. He experimented once more with flowers and shrubs; he espaliered fruit trees, and persuaded gardens and orchards to yield luscious produce. He enjoyed matching his wits against nature, trying to lengthen the bearing seasons and sometimes he succeeded in stretching out the yield all the year round.

But it was not enough. He was an industrious man by nature, and the slower pace did not really suit him. He did not live very long, and my mother went to live with Jean-Marie, who was now married and in business for himself.

Things had also changed for me. The war and the sudden freedom everywhere which followed it had given me a personal freedom I had never dreamed of. I told myself I didn't want to marry, at least for some time, and I decided to move back into the city and be on my own. Lyon was crowded with workers, eager for a comfortable lodging, and it seemed to me that in this situation I might find a way to use the skills my mother had taught me.

I leased a large apartment and rented out several rooms, which gave me an income. It was not precisely a *pension*, because I did not ordinarily furnish meals with the rooms. Occasionally, however, I cooked a meal for a girl lodger if she was trying to save money while she made a career. I would serve her a plain omelette with the youngest of green beans and plenty of good crusty bread. All in all, my experiment went well.

One day, after what I thought was a surprising passage of time, another letter came from Joannes. Was I still single? If so, would I marry him now? There was no need to reply in writing, because he was coming to Lyon on a combined business and pleasure trip, and he would hear my answer in person.

I think I knew at that moment what my answer would be. We were married in November 1931, and left at once for our new home in New York. I found it a strange and frightening place. I was protected from the consequences of being unable to speak any English by the kindness of our best friends, a French couple. The wife, who was a daughter of the Baronne de Bournat, understood my absolute terror of everything in this new country, including going out into the streets by myself, and she kept me almost constant company.

The more protected I was, the more timid I became. I waited to do the marketing until Joannes came home from work to our apartment in Brooklyn. But he had the wisdom to see that if I were not forced a little I would become a permanent baby, and in any case he wanted to move to Manhattan so he would be nearer his factory.

In our new apartment I did my best to break the dependency which had made me so much a prisoner, but I still avoided going to market alone. The apartment was on a high floor, and I could decorate outdoors as well as inside since there was a fine terrace. I arranged the plants and flowers my father had taught me to grow. But still I did not learn English. Perhaps I was protesting subconsciously against being uprooted from my beloved Lyon, and hoped to return. Joannes caught me sitting on the terrace, watching with wistful eyes the great ocean liners as they swung out into the Hudson on their way to Europe, and he arranged a little present for me—a short visit home to see my mother.

I was so happy to be on that ship, and excited to discover that Monsieur Herriot, by then a famous statesman, was a fellow passenger. Famous or not, I had carried many a *poulet Marie* to his table and I felt no shyness about going up and speaking to him when I encountered him on deck. He remembered me well, and greeted me kindly. We met often during the voyage, and he spoke affectionately of my father.

It was exciting, too, to be home in Lyon again, but after the first flush had worn away, I asked myself, "Romaine Champion, what are you doing here in France when your husband is three thousand miles away in New York?" I sailed for home again at the first opportunity.

When Joannes met me at the pier, I told him at once that I was cured of my timidity and foolish fears. I would learn to speak English quickly, I told him, and I would go about the city bravely by myself. Somehow I had forgotten the terror of marketing, because when he announced a day or two later, taking me at my word, that he would no longer be doing the marketing with me, I was shocked.

I cried and stormed, but this time he did not give in. He did something more sensible. In the kindest way, he wrote out the marketing lists for me, one column in French and the English equivalents opposite, taking the trouble to spell them out phonetically. By concentrating hard, I could manage to pronounce them.

I do not know how I got to the market on that first day, how I made myself understood, or what I carried home—but Joannes was pleased. "I knew you could do it," he said. "You will have no more trouble now." Since nothing seemed to turn out wrong in the kitchen that night, I felt a peace I had not known since I came to the United States.

From that night on, I began to acclimate myself to America. Now that I was no longer afraid, I could enjoy my home the more, and life went beautifully until, without warning, came the greatest blow of all. Joannes had always been the strongest and healthiest of men, but for a long time he had been working day and night—much of the time I worked beside him—to make his struggling textile business a success. He never got enough rest, yet he was always in good spirits.

One May morning he put a boutonniere of violets from one of my window boxes into his lapel, waved good-by to me, and left for the factory. A few hours later the doorbell rang. One of the men from the factory stood there, trying to tell me something. He was having a hard time forming the words. Joannes had suffered a heart attack. He was unconscious when I got to the hospital and died soon after. I had the comfort of knowing he had not suffered, but all I could think was, How does it happen I am still living?

In a haze of misery I went back to Lyon, but I felt myself a stranger there. It was no longer my home, and I could not bring myself to look for work. I fled back to New York once more. In its empty way it was the nearest thing to home because it was there my husband was at rest.

I groped around for a time, thinking of my skills and wondering how I could turn them into some trade that would occupy my mind and earn a little money. The thing I knew most about was the restaurant business, but strangely enough, I did not give it a thought. Millinery was the best prospect, I decided. I even made a trip to Paris and brought back some models. To my surprise, I found some promise of success right at my doorstep. Ladies in the elevator of my apartment house stared appreciatively at my hats, and several times, fearing there was a possibility they might be snatched from my head, I promised to make stitch-for-stitch copies. I put prices on them which were formidable, yet the ladies scarcely seemed to listen. It was only important to them that they should acquire bits of French chic to wear to lunch in fashionable restaurants and make their friends jealous.

However, I could see no real satisfaction in making hats for women driven by social anxiety. Besides, even with the high prices, I had to put in too much work, and too much cash into what proved to be a poor partnership. My husband's estate was evaporating at an alarming rate, and I knew I must find something that would ease my bank account as well as my mind.

At best it was not a favorable time for an inexperienced Frenchwoman with few friends in a strange country and with the ability to say scarcely more than "please" and "thank you" in English, to go into business for herself. The war had already begun in Europe, and America was in a state of limited emergency. I had seen with my own eyes what war did to business.

Nevertheless I compelled myself to walk, day after day and mile after mile, through the streets of New York, looking rather vaguely, I am afraid, for some location where perhaps I could take a small risk in business. I knew that the only really salable talent I had was preparing food, but I had no intention of trying a restaurant which would serve entire meals. That would require a large kitchen range, help, pots and pans, a daily merchandise of fresh meats, vegetables and fruits, dishes, silverware, tables, and tablecloths—altogether too large an outlay for one with almost no capital and less English.

I kept on walking and looking; it was better than doing nothing, letting the days slip like sand through my fingers. One day I happened to pass east of Lexington Avenue into a street from which I expected nothing, but glancing up suddenly, I noticed a small shop. It was very small indeed. A sign swung outside with a rusty, scraping sound, and the wooden form of a boot hung over the door. *Sabotier*, I thought, not knowing the English word "cobbler." The street number amused me: it was 137½. I had never known they came in halves.

I walked along for a few yards but something seemed to twitch at my sleeve and I turned back. Peering in the window I saw that the shoe-mending business took up half of a long, narrow shop. Over the other half dangled a sign proclaiming it vacant. Would that be room enough for me to have a small place of business? Perhaps I could sell pastries to be taken out; I knew that Americans had an attachment for pastries almost as great as the Viennese. Would there, perhaps, be room enough for two or three large tables where afternoon strollers could come to sit and consume petits fours, *chocolat*, tea, and coffee?

Curiosity carried me in to speak to the shoemender. Naturally he glanced first at my shoes and found them in perfect order. "Good day, madame," he said politely. "Something?"

He was tall and very dark, with Greek features. I saw that
he was a contented and good-humored man. While we talked,
his hands continued their work very rapidly. My questions
were in limited English, and French; his answers were in
slightly less limited English, and Greek. If he did not approve
of French pastries side by side with leather and shoe polish,
he did not say so. Certainly, he told me, the owner was hoping
for a tenant for the other half of this place. One need only
make a businesslike impression, arrange the terms of lease,
pay a month's rent in advance, put up a sign OPENING SOON,
clean the premises, and perhaps touch them up with a little
paint, then all would be ready. For what? French pastries,
did Madame say? *Chocolat,* tea, or coffee—no wines or
liquor?

I assured him that was exactly what I had in mind, and I
could see it pleased him. The Greeks have a natural sweet
tooth, and use large amounts of honey in their pastries. Perhaps mine would make us good neighbors. My spirits began
to rise.

The owner seemed satisfied with me and came himself to
take down the FOR RENT sign, lending me his fountain pen to
sign the lease. To pay the first month's rent I had to pawn
some jewelry, and for a moment I faltered. My husband had
given me that jewelry, and it was possible I would never be
successful enough to redeem it. But I could almost hear
Joannes telling me that independence and a business to occupy my mind was better than a few diamonds and sapphires.
The owner got his rent and gave me a key.

I found a young man in the neighborhood to make the two
signs I would need, OPENING SOON and SALON DE THÉ. He was
very cheerful and explained that he was pleased to have my
order because any day now, as soon as he had earned enough
money to pay for his one-way, third-class passage, he was leav-

ing for Paris to become a painter. Until he could sail, he was making ends meet by lettering signs. After all, he pointed out, Toulouse-Lautrec had started by painting posters for the Moulin Rouge.

He considered OPENING SOON nothing at all, a mere exercise which he dashed off quickly. But for SALON DE THÉ he carefully made me a sample, and complimented me on my selection of the name. As he worked, he practiced the French phrases he thought he would need when he got to Paris.

The shop was scrubbed and touched up with fresh paint, rose and turquoise. I chose those because they were my birthstone colors, and might bring me luck. I brought in some flowering plants and bits of bric-a-brac typical of France. Behind a cretonne curtain, I fitted a tiny space with a double hot plate and, in front, arranged several small tables with composition tops, making tablecloths unnecessary. Then, with enough tea plates, cups, saucers, and plated silverware for serving, I was ready. At last I had something to occupy my desolate mind.

At the end of the first day's business, I had taken in exactly three dollars. That was little enough, considering what had been expended to earn it, but to a Frenchwoman and a Lyonnaise, who had been brought up to respect even the centime, three dollars was three dollars.

Business soon began to improve, however. People would put their heads in the door and exclaim, "Only someone French would be able to make a business in a shop so small." Then they would come in and buy pastries to eat at the tables or take out. I was beginning to be known in the neighborhood, and people who lived nearby began to make it a habit to drop in. Some were celebrities; others were about to be. They brought their friends, and their friends brought *their* friends.

One day a lady came in briskly and announced, "I am

Clementine Paddleford, from the *Herald Tribune.*" I told her politely that with my poor English I tried to read her column.

"I have come to see this hole-in-the-wall of yours, to interview you about what you are doing here," Miss Paddleford said, "and I have brought a photographer to take a picture of you in it."

"Oh, no, madame," I said, terrified. Not knowing anything about publicity and its power to make people buy, I did not understand her firmness. "I do not wish my picture taken," I said, just as firmly. "Will people buy from me because they see how I look? I think not. So if you please, madame, no pictures. Thank you so much for your trouble to come here, madame, but no picture."

"No picture, no story, madame," she said, still very firm.

"I am sorry. *Au revoir, madame.*"

"Well, if that's the way you feel," she said, and went away, taking her photographer.

I told a few people about the incident, and they laughed and said I had made a very big mistake, that I had deliberately killed the goose that quite possibly would have laid a golden egg. Still I did not understand. In Lyon no photographer ever came to take my father's picture so that we would get customers. What brought people to our restaurant was the excellent food and the pleasant environment.

It was true that my Salon de Thé offered delicious pastries and beverages. I adopted a few little personal trademarks, such as lace jabots with my black dresses, and always a little knot of artificial violets worn under the chin. One patron used to bring his friends, always saying to them as they came in the door, "I want you to see La Demoiselle de Lyon. She is so French, with her jabots and her violets." Some of my customers called me the Lady of the Violets.

My Greek neighbor soon had the habit of stopping his

pounding and mending and coming into my place now and then to buy himself a *cornet à la crème*. Plainly he thought himself in great good luck to have acquired someone like me in the other half of the shop.

I had never worked harder in my life, and it was not long before I had all the patrons I could take care of. Sometimes the last of them did not wish to leave until nearly midnight. I would go home extremely tired but happy that at last I was on my way to success. I grieved for Joannes, but I believed he would have been proud of me.

In time I began to open on Sundays, and many people came from church for breakfast or luncheon. I made up a luncheon menu of sandwiches, making them with French bread split lengthwise, and using my imagination to make a variety of fillings. I remembered, too, how we had made use of the pumpkin back in Lyon. I had noticed that in America people seemed to think of pumpkin only at Thanksgiving and Christmas, when they bought it as a habit and made it into pies. We had prepared something of the kind in Lyon, a *gâteau de courge*, something more like a cake than a pie, made of pumpkin and cooked in the oven as a dessert. But we also used pumpkin to make a very good soup, and because people came to my place quite hungry sometimes, I thought I would put pumpkin soup on my menu.

This is the way I make it. Peel the pumpkin, cut it in small pieces, and cook it in salted water until it is soft. Drain, then mash it as if you were making mashed potatoes. Add a big piece of butter and one cup of heavy cream. Sometimes, if I do not have enough pumpkin, I add some potatoes, which lightens the taste, making it a little more subtle than the pure pumpkin.

Gradually luncheon at Madame Romaine's, especially on Sundays, became a little novelty. People requested French bread in the long loaves to carry home with them from this *coin de Paris.* Many of my patrons were themselves French, people who had fled from France when the Germans came. Some were members of the French nobility.

And fortunately for me, Miss Paddleford did not take what I had said as necessarily final. One day she came back again. I cannot say she argued or even persuaded, but although I still felt a little shy and ridiculous, I let her photographer take the picture. She wrote very nicely about me in the *Herald Tribune,* mentioning not only the rose and turquoise of my decor, the growing plants and the fresh flowers on the tables, and the bibelots to remind people of France and Lyon, but also the fruit jams I had for sale on my counter, and what intrigued her more, my jams made from vegetables—peas, turnips, green tomatoes and red, even potatoes. I colored the potato jam with a little sweet liqueur, green or coral, and patrons bought it, enchanted, because it gave the jam the surprising taste of *marrons glacés.*

Miss Paddleford mentioned that, although I did not serve that delicacy of Lyon, *quenelles de brochet,* in the shop, I would sometimes cook them to order for those who wished to serve that unique dish at home. She also told about my *bugnes de Lyon,* which are thin strips of pastry fried to a beautiful brown in deep fat.

Now people in numbers put their heads in the door every day, calling out, "Well, this must be the hole-in-the-wall where Miss Paddleford said we must come to eat pastry." Now I knew how wrong I had been to tilt my nose at her photographer, but I had not realized that I was living in a country where, if you turn your head away from publicity, the public may turn its head away from you.

Probably my best customers at the time—they came every day for a year—were Don Loper and George Lloyd. Mr. Loper was then a dancer in night-club and Broadway shows: now, as everyone knows, he is one of the noted couturiers and interior decorators in Hollywood. He and Mr. Lloyd used to come every day at 4 o'clock to eat croissants and drink *chocolat*, but occasionally Mr. Loper would ask for an omelette.

Sometimes these two gentlemen came alone, but most of the time they brought their friends. One day Mr. Lloyd, who was then an actor and remained my great friend for twenty years, introduced me to a friend of his, Miss Thelma Schnee, who was appearing in *The Corn Is Green* with Ethel Barrymore. She was a charming and unassuming girl who was so enchanted with my place immediately that she, too, became a regular customer. Often she brought members of her family. They made a little joke, saying that if they could not look forward to coming to my place, they wouldn't know what to do with themselves.

At first Miss Schnee took only a pastry, with coffee or tea, but one day she came in at an off-hour exclaiming, "Oh, madame, I am so hungry. I do love eggs. Could you possibly give me an omelette?"

In my refrigerator was an extra box of eggs which I had bought to take home. I heard myself saying, "Certainly, mademoiselle, it will take just a minute."

To be exact, it would take two minutes. For a plain omelette, two minutes is just right. The reason for this is that you must not abuse the egg with cooking, for then it will respond by abusing the stomach. In any event, Miss Schnee was delighted to find that she could have an omelette in my place.

In this unexpected and wholly unplanned fashion, omelettes began as my *spécialité de la maison*, although I did nothing more about them for a time. Well, not exactly nothing. Miss Schnee came in every day, asking for an omelette, and every time she had one somebody at another table would be sure to see it and exclaim, "Oh, madame, it looks so good —can I have one too?" A few also said, "Will you tell me, madame, how I can make such an omelette? Whenever I try, it turns out to be a horror!" Then someone else would say, "I can make a plain omelette but not one with mushrooms. Will you show me how to do that?"

Nevertheless I put off considering omelettes as a regular part of my Salon de Thé. But sometimes when I got home at night and lay in bed, going over in my mind what had happened that day, I thought of those omelettes again and asked myself if I should take them more seriously. I would not give up my pastries and beverages, or the jams, French chocolates, and imported delicacies I sold from my counter, but perhaps I should listen to the suggestions of people who wanted omelettes.

Then something occurred, an incident I would not have dreamed of, which put me into the omelette business in the most unexpected way. Not far from my shop there is a night club called the Blue Angel, and one day I had a telephone call from my good friend Mr. Jacoby, the owner, who often came into my place. He said he would like to discuss a matter with me, and I told him I would listen.

"Romaine," Mr. Jacoby said, "I would like you to help me furnish my customers with a novelty."

"A novelty? What would that be?"

"I would like you to come here in the late evening and make omelettes for the after-theater crowd. I have heard there is nothing like your omelettes this side of France. Our customers would not only enjoy them, they would find them a pleasant change from the usual menu."

"I don't know," I said doubtfully.

"I thought we could have a *table roulante*," Mr. Jacoby went on, unperturbed. "You know, the kind used in some restaurants for taking roast beef to be carved at the tables. You would be able to make their omelettes right in front of them."

"Oh, no, that could not be done at all."

"Why not?"

"One must make the omelette quickly, in an open pan which must be hot. Butter might spatter from the pan onto a lady's dress. Very likely it would be her new Mainbocher, and you would have a large bill at the dry cleaner's if you did not have a lawsuit instead." That was true, but it was also true I would have been frightened to death to make an omelette in front of a customer.

"Well—" Mr. Jacoby paused doubtfully.

"No, a *table roulante* would not be for me," I said, but I did not want to let it go at that. His idea was interesting. "The only way to do as you ask," I said, "would be to make the omelettes in the kitchen where the rest of the menu is made. The kitchen is the proper place for cooking an omelette."

"Then you'll do it, Romaine?" he exclaimed.

"I will try, and we shall see what happens," I said.

That was how I began cooking late at night in the Blue Angel, after my own place was closed. I did not know how successful I was at this occupation until one evening when the maître d' came rushing into the kitchen himself, with an order for omelettes *fines herbes*. "Do the best you've ever done in your life!" he shouted in his excitement. As it is my rule to try at any time to do the best I have ever done in my life, I said calmly, "Who is this for, *alors*, a king?"

"It has to be perfect!" the maître d' threw over his shoulder as he rushed out again.

I made the omelettes and sent them up. About an hour later a waiter came in saying, "Put on a fresh apron and go upstairs to be thanked."

"Thanked? By whom?"

"You'll see," he smiled.

The maître d' led me to a table and I saw that everyone in the room was staring at the scene. Making an impressive bow, the maître d' said, "Your Royal Highness, Madame la Duchesse, I present the author of your omelettes, Madame Romaine."

"Your omelettes are delicious," said a warm, feminine American voice. "We have never had better," said a slightly high-pitched male English voice.

"Thank you, sir, madame," I heard myself saying. "You are kind to say so." I went back to the kitchen thinking that, if the Duke and Duchess of Windsor liked my omelettes, others would. Perhaps I had better begin to think about making a menu of them for my shop. I remembered how, at our restaurant in Lyon, an omelette would often be ordered as a main dish. Already I was thinking of names to give them.

Meanwhile, I went on making omelettes for customers at the Blue Angel, thousands of them for people from all over the world. But after six months of it I could begin to feel a strain, which was only natural since I worked in my own place from about nine-thirty in the morning until nearly ten o'clock at night, and then in the Blue Angel until closing time, at three o'clock. Besides, my own business was increasing and it needed all my time and energies. Mr. Jacoby was most understanding, and of course we parted good friends.

As more and more people found my little hole-in-the-wall, I invented new omelettes and added them to my menu. By this time the United States was in the war, supplies were becoming very hard to get, and it was easier to concentrate on omelettes than to carry on as I had before.

I had been in my shop for about five years when a real crisis occurred, which made me fear it had all been for nothing. The building I was in was about to be torn down, and I was notified that I would have to move. As you may imagine, I was in a state of nerves. I remembered how hard it had been for me to find this place, and now, with the war, it was almost impossible to find any place, large or small. Many people I knew were literally homeless, moving from hotel to hotel, unless they could leave the city or move in temporarily with a friend or relative. Store space was just as hard to get because building had almost stopped. I looked all over town and found nothing.

My Greek neighbor had left some time before, and one morning the hairdresser who had taken over his half told me that a place called The Basket Dinner, at 133 East 56th, just down the street, was about to close. It was a small place run by two women who cooked chicken dinners to be taken out, but now with the war they had to go out of business. A miracle! Here was a store just the size I wanted, and in the same neighborhood.

I hurried over and began the negotiations at once. In order to get the store I had to buy out the business, and that was more expense than I had counted on, but I was too desperate to argue very much. Soon after, in April 1945, I moved in, and I have been there ever since. It was larger than the original place, seating about twenty persons. The kitchen was larger, too, although any other restaurant owner would have considered it a closet. It was quite large enough for me.

Often I have heard friends tell me how foolish I am to stay in such small quarters when business is always so good, how I should open a much larger place, where I could serve drinks and meals as well. I do not think so. I think I am right to keep my place unique, devoted to omelettes. I have seen too many successful small restaurants fail when their owners were persuaded to enlarge them.

"Madame," they have told me often, "you can make a fortune quickly and retire if you will only expand." But I am not greedy, and I have never wanted to retire. What would I do all day? I have been busy all my life since I was a young girl, and while I know I cannot work this way forever, the time is not yet. And of one thing I am certain. The customers would not come as they do now if I myself was not able to cook all the omelettes, as I do now, and always have. My patrons come because it is I, Madame Romaine, who cook for them, not some mysterious chef hidden away in a kitchen behind a large dining room.

No, I shall cook omelettes until I am at last tired of it, or too old to work so hard any more. Then I will stop, but not before. Meanwhile, in this book, I will tell you what I know about making omelettes, so that if the day arrives when there is no longer a Madame Romaine's to come to, you will be able to take this book from your shelf and say, "Voilà! I will make my own!"

CHAPTER 2

How to Cook an Omelette

What is an omelette?

"But, madame," you say, "everyone knows what an omelette is."

I will tell you something. Everyone does *not* know. I can prove it with a story which has always been one of my favorites. One day, after omelettes had become my specialty, I saw two women peering in the doorway of my place, after the last luncheon customer had gone. It was one of the first warm days of early spring, and since I did not then have air conditioning, the door was standing open.

I looked twice at these ladies because something about them made me feel sympathetic. They looked the way I felt when I was a stranger in New York; probably, I thought, they came from a village somewhere up in the state. They were in their early thirties, wearing little cotton print dresses. The city was interesting to them, but they did not feel sure about it.

One of them caught my eye and said rather shyly, "It says you only serve omelettes and salad." She glanced at her friend

and added, "What is an omelette? I never saw one." I saw
that she was serious, and I could not have been more surprised. I thought all Americans knew omelettes, the way all
French know truffles.

I described my plain omelette because it was a good il-
lustration, in no way difficult to understand.

"Oh," they said together, looking at each other again, then
shaking their heads. "Well, thank you," they said, and backed
away from my door. I returned to my kitchen, shaking my
own head a little. I thought I had learned everything from
my customers, but it seemed there was still something to
be learned.

Perhaps there are those among my readers who are also
strangers to the omelette, although I cannot imagine why
they would have bought this book. I suspect there may be
many others who believe they know more about omelettes
than they do, because the dish is, after all, not uncommon in
America. It may be well, then, for me to give you an introduction to the omelette; to know it well calls for understanding
as well as simple acquaintance.

What, may I ask again, is an omelette? It is a little like
scrambled eggs (but not quite) folded into a sort of self-
envelope. Its variations occur when you tuck some special
kind of filling inside. My menu lists more than five hundred
of these variations, and I am sure there are a great many
others.

Everyone who cooks should know how to do an omelette.
It is something one may serve at any time, either with plan-
ning in advance or at the last moment when circumstances
require something quickly from the kitchen. The omelette is
such an accommodating dish. It can be served by itself, with
only a salad and a glass of wine; it has its own dignity as an
entree in a larger meal; and it will also do for a dessert, al-

though that is a special problem I will say more about later.

An omelette can be simple or it can be complicated. The latter type may be made with certain meats, vegetables, and nuts, and cognac; or with chicken, *foie gras*, chestnuts, almonds, and an Armagnac sauce; or with beef, *foie gras*, truffles, mushrooms, walnuts, and a Courvoisier sauce; or, indeed, with endless other ingredients and variations. The best part of it is that anyone can learn to do even the most complicated ones.

I learned about the wonderful variety of omelettes from my mother. Like a magpie, she collected the smallest scraps of anything usable. Any leftovers from our midday meal in the restaurant were saved up, and when the day's work was over, they were often materials for a beautiful omelette which was our evening meal. The French, I might add, customarily eat their big meal in the middle of the day; the evening meal is light but sufficient, usually a soup, an omelette, perhaps, with a bit of cheese and fruit, and of course wine. A Frenchman in the most modest circumstances eating such a meal need not envy even the President of France, because he knows that most Frenchmen of every class are eating essentially the same kind of evening supper.

Wherever the omelette is cooked, in France or in America or elsewhere, it is no more important than the pan in which it is cooked. I must tell you positively that the wrong pan can ruin the omelette. It should be of medium weight, first of all. Never use a thick iron skillet because it will be too heavy to handle and will not work properly. It should also be small, no more than six or eight inches at the top, with sides slanting out, not in, so that the omelette, when it is finished, will slide more easily.

If an omelette in the pan starts to stick at the bottom, here is a tip: tilt the pan toward you as much as you can as you hold the handle, then take a piece of butter or fat and put it in the upper side of the pan, letting it run under the omelette. Then shake the pan and everything will be all right.

I deplore such fancy devices as the aluminum omelette pan, oval-shaped and hinged down the center in two halves. The omelette is cooked in two portions, then folded together in two layers. This builds the omelette high, rather like a hat built of layers of tulle. This may be all right for people who like to play while they cook, but my advice, from experience, is to use an iron pan. It can be made of stainless steel, of course, if you prefer it, but personally I like iron, and, as I have said, it must be lighter than the usual cast-iron pan. If you insist on using aluminum, you will find that your omelette is likely to become dry, or burn.

If you do not have an omelette pan and are going to buy one, here are some things to keep in mind. You must prepare a new pan. It has to be seasoned before it can be used. Of course, nowadays you can buy a pan already seasoned, but it is not always the right size. However, seasoning a pan is easy. Put some oil (any oil you have) into the pan so that it covers the bottom. Warm it up slowly and turn the pan occasionally so that the oil coats the sides. Let the pan become hot, then take it off the fire and let it cool off. Perform this operation two or three times and let the oil stand in it overnight.

Next day warm the pan up, pour the oil out (you may use it again), and wipe your pan dry. It is now ready to make an omelette. Remember, never wash an omelette pan. If for any reason washing is unavoidable, afterward turn the pan upside down over the fire and turn up the flame. When the pan has become very hot, take it off the fire and let it cool a little. Put some oil in it and warm it up for a few minutes. Then wipe it dry, and it should be as good as new.

There is one important rule: never, *never* wash your omelette pan. After it has been used, wipe it lightly. A paper towel will do, or a soft cloth. The pan should always be a little oily, but of course never greasy. And never use your omelette pan for anything except omelettes. For omelettes with fillings using fish, keep a separate pan to be used only for that purpose, and the same rule applies to sweet omelettes.

My mother, I recall, cleaned her pans with salt, but also with very fine steel wool. I do something else. I invert the pan over the stove and turn the flame up high, letting the pan become very hot. Then, after it cools, I put some oil in the bottom and leave it overnight. That is all you need to do. Never scrape the pan with a knife or any sharp instrument if something sticks to the cooking surface; just get out your salt and steel wool.

If you take care of your omelette pan, it will improve with age. It will begin to look pretty black, but it will be an honorable black. In France, when such a pan has been in long use, we call it *cullotté*, meaning that it has become colored by serving us well.

So much for the pan. Now let us consider the eggs. I have heard people say, "I never use anything but brown eggs," to which someone is always certain to reply, "Mon dieu, I would not think of using anything but white eggs." I have even heard that you can tell people are from Boston because they will use only brown eggs, while New Yorkers demand white eggs. I can see no reason for such nonsense. An egg is an egg. Is a blond girl less human than a brunette? I do not think so. If there is a reason for this prejudice about eggs, other than some kind of mythology, perhaps it is because white eggs seem to look nicer than brown ones. I notice that when food is arranged to be photographed in color for a magazine advertisement, the eggs are always white. But I will tell you something. I always use brown eggs to make my sauces, because brown egg yolks are more yellow and give the sauces a richer shade.

There is one thing about omelettes with which some Americans do not agree. In France we believe it is necessary that the omelette should be *baveuse*—that is, creamy in its center. As in all French cooking, there is a principle behind this conviction. As anyone who has cooked or even scrambled eggs knows, the risk in preparing eggs is overcooking, which will only make them very dry and tough, and certainly not welcome to the palate. Cooking the omelette with attention to keeping the center slightly moist—not raw—is a way of presenting the eggs at their best. Now and then, inevitably it seems, I encounter a patron's demand for a dry omelette, well done. To my mind, such an omelette can only be a disaster. But I do not argue. I swallow my dismay and hope the patron will someday see his error and give up his barbarism.

Another form of criminality is to use a mechanical beater to make an omelette. A fork is the thing. I will agree, it is harder to do the beating by hand, and I do not know why it is that some eggs require more beating than others, but they do. But if you do not care enough to put in whatever time and labor is necessary to prepare eggs in the way that is best, then you should not be thinking about making an omelette at all.

For myself, I beat the eggs twenty-five to thirty seconds. "But, madame," you say, "I do not cook with a stopwatch!" Nor do I. The point is to beat your eggs very briskly until they are well mixed, and my experience tells me that to do this takes beating them quite hard for about twenty-five to thirty seconds, as I have said. That means about thirty to forty-five beatings. You will have to learn to do this from your own experience and practice. If you do not beat enough, the eggs will not be mixed properly; if too much, they will be too thin, like water, and watery eggs are never agreeable in omelettes.

Do not imagine that you can make one big omelette and cut it up for several guests. You can do it, but it will not be a true omelette of superior quality. It is a mark of attention to the guest to give him his own omelette. There is also a practical side to this nicety. Suppose you have made a large omelette with mushrooms, or *foie gras*, or cheese, or artichokes, and then one of your guests, as it happens, cannot stand mushrooms, or *foie gras*, or that kind of cheese, or even artichokes? If that does not encourage you to make individual omelettes, I will tell you something else. Making a large one is much harder to do.

Having learned about pans and eggs, and their proper combination, we are ready for the cooking. I will only observe, before getting down to actual preparation, that I am not so reckless as to pretend that an omelette is thinning. On the other hand, not all omelettes are fattening. It depends in large part on what is in them. People who are too thin would do well to eat omelettes; it will help them put on weight in a nourishing way.

Now to the stove!

There is a way to approach it mentally. One must be realistic about omelette cookery. Many people think it difficult, and so it will always be for people who have no knowledge of cooking. For them it will be as difficult as anything they will every try. But for those who already know how to cook, it should not be at all difficult. However, it *is* a little tricky and practice is the only way to arrive at success.

As everyone knows, good cooks are people who do something more than follow a recipe literally. They know what it means when a recipe calls for "a pinch" of this, or "a soup-

çon" of that, or something else "browned in butter." Beyond
that, they understand that a cultivated sense of taste is a
prerequisite to good cooking. For such people, who can cook
but still have never been able to make an omelette properly,
my explanation and a little practice will enable them to do as
well as I do.

As you practice, keep in mind that you must master three
fundamental things: putting in the proper amount of butter;
keeping the flame at the proper height, not too high or too
low; and beating the eggs in the way I have described. With
these fundamentals thoroughly learned, the rest will be easy,
and you will see that an omelette is almost like scrambled
eggs, but not quite. By leaving the eggs in the pan five seconds
longer, a kind of envelope is formed, which is your omelette.

An omelette is made very quickly. It does not take more
than a minute to make an individual plain omelette, and
no more than two or three minutes if ingredients to make
a filling are added. The omelette must be made at the last
minute, when you are ready to eat it. Never prepare the eggs
too far in advance. Some ingredients, of course, have to be
precooked, like potatoes, asparagus, spinach, and cauliflower;
but tomatoes, eggplant, and such vegetables are cooked when
you make the omelette. And always remember—you can wait
for an omelette, but the omelette will not wait for you. As it
gets cold, it becomes tougher, and so it must be eaten warm.
Master the plain omelette first, and the others will be easy.

This is how I do it.

PLAIN OMELETTE   Take your pan and put it on the
fire over a low flame so that it will warm up. In it put a well-
rounded tablespoon of butter. I like sweet butter, which we
are accustomed to use in France. But the important thing
is not to skimp on it, otherwise the omelette will stick to
the bottom of the pan.

While the butter is melting, slowly break 3 whole eggs in a bowl, add salt and pepper to taste (I never measure anything), and add a tablespoon of water from the faucet. Never use milk or cream. Now beat your eggs briskly in the manner I have described.

When the eggs are beaten, turn the flame high under the pan, and when the butter is a nice light brown color, pour the eggs into it. With the handle of the pan in your left hand and a fork in your right hand, bring the eggs from the sides of the pan to the center. Do this quickly, meanwhile shaking the pan so that the eggs will not stick to the bottom. Keep on lifting the eggs with the fork, almost as if you were doing scrambled eggs, until all the liquid runs under. In about five more seconds the envelope will form, as I have described.

Now transfer the omelette quickly to a warm plate. To do this, lift the edge of the omelette nearer you, fold it in half and turn onto the plate.

This plain omelette should not take more than a minute to make—the quicker, the better. Because I am so experienced with it, I make mine on a very high flame, but I recommend a medium flame for those who are learning.

Practice is the only way to make a perfect omelette, I repeat. Even after you have followed my directions, you may say, "I *still* can't make a decent omelette." But you must have confidence in yourself, as my mother used to say to me. Try it ten times, twenty times, even fifty times, until you have mastered the art.

FILLED OMELETTES When it comes to making omelettes with fillings, I have my own method, which I do not think is found in any cookbook. Indeed, it will horrify many cooks, I am sure, but it is the method I learned from my mother long ago, and I make all my omelettes that way, with only a few exceptions. Most recipes tell you to pour the eggs

in the pan, and when they are a little coagulated, pour in the
fillings. I do just the opposite. I add the fillings to the hot
butter in the pan, sauté them a bit, and then put the eggs
on top. Keep lifting with the fork, permitting the eggs to run
underneath. When the omelette is folded, the filling will be
in the middle.

How well I remember my mother doing just that when she
was making our evening meal—putting the leftovers from
midday, whether they were meat or vegetables, into the pan
and warming them up in the butter, then throwing some
eggs on top to make a nice omelette. It was this recollection
which gave me the idea for all those meat and vegetable
omelettes on my menu.

Every morning I come early to my restaurant and cook
what I will need that day. When everything is cooked, I put
it in small containers on my table and use whatever is needed
from this collection to make the omelette called for. I simply
take whatever meats or vegetables are needed, toss them
in hot butter, turn them around for a few seconds, pour the
egg on top, and finish the omelette. You can do the same
thing, by saving leftovers, as my mother did.

When you want to make a complicated omelette—that is,
with three or four ingredients in it—don't do it at the last
minute or you will have too much work. Prepare your vegetables or meat in the morning, or even the day before, so that
when the mealtime comes you will have only the omelette
to do.

To show you what can be done, suppose you have chicken
one day with an accompaniment of string beans, or peas, or
spinach. Keep a little of the chicken, and a little of each of
the vegetables if you can, and next day you will have all the
materials for omelettes. Keep the liver, too, and you will have
an even greater variety possible. And what a variety! You

can have a chicken omelette, or a chicken-liver omelette, or either one with all the vegetables, or one vegetable with the chicken omelette and another with the livers. Whatever you are having for dinner, in fact, you can always put a little aside for next day's omelette, creating new ones to suit your own taste. That is what I have done, and it is why I have so many different omelettes.

If you examine my menu, lengthy as it is (553 omelettes), and containing more varieties than most people ever imagine for their own kitchens, it nevertheless omits many ingredients which are entirely possible as fillings, things like shrimp, or mussels, or oysters, or game. Those I omit are not included because they do not appeal to everyone, or—like game—because they are difficult to find, or else because the preparation takes a little too long and I do not have the time. But anyone cooking at home can use these ingredients and others very easily.

I have often been asked why I do not make soufflés, and why I do not do a jam omelette. The answers are simple. I do not make soufflés because I do not have the facilities for them, and in any case they are not really omelettes. As for sweet omelettes, I take the French view that they are desserts, or to be served after the theater. My omelettes are the main dish of a luncheon, or any other meal, and I am not open after the theater—consequently, no sweet omelettes.

Some of my patrons do not understand why they cannot have a dessert omelette as a main course, but then, there are many things about food which some of my American customers do not seem to grasp easily. For example, in my earlier days with the restaurant I used to serve a rum omelette, and there were customers who asked for a salad with it. How horrible! It is as barbaric as the customer who will eat a fish omelette with a wine sauce and insist on drinking a *chocolat* with it. Awful!

It is well to remember that omelettes come in three quite different classifications, as follows: omelette *garnie*, meaning served with vegetables around it as a garnish; omelette *fourrée*, meaning one made with a filling; and the omelette *sucrée*, which is the sweet omelette made with sugar, fruits, or jams. I suppose the plain omelette is in a class by itself.

In the recipes which follow, please remember that omelettes are all done the same way basically, so I will not repeat every time how much butter you should put in the pan, because it will be exactly the same for each one. In the variations of cheese omelette, the quantities will always be the same, but of course you can add more if it suits your taste. You may also make it with different kinds of cheese, if you like. Many people like Parmesan, for example. My mother used only Swiss (Gruyère, as we called it) and so it is natural that I use Swiss too. But again, use your own taste and imagination.

One other explanation. What I call French bacon (*lard*) is probably known to you as salt pork, and what is called lard here we know as white fat in France. The salt pork must not be too fat and not too lean, but nicely half and half. It is better than smoked bacon, because the latter will kill every other taste, while salt pork adds some flavor without taking it away from any other ingredient. Lardons are small pieces of bacon or salt pork.

On to the kitchen, then. The recipes you can make there, at least the ones I have made, will be found in the following pages. Only your own imagination governs the number you will be able to add to them. As for my own, I guarantee them. Fifty thousand customers *can't* be wrong.

❧ ❧ ❧   CHAPTER 3

Omelette Recipes

Before you begin, a few words of explanation about these recipes. They are not exactly like the ones you are accustomed to in standard cookbooks, since the omelettes are all variations on a theme. In giving the various recipes for chicken omelettes, for example, it will not be necessary to repeat the amount of chicken because it will be the same for every omelette in which chicken is the base. The same will be true of other basic ingredients. If there are exceptions, they will be noted.

If you are not confident about cooking some of the ingredients right in the omelette pan—croutons and bacon, for example—I suggest you make them separately in another pan. Still, the croutons are made so quickly that you should be able to do them in the omelette pan. Experience will teach you what other ingredients may be used.

When I say sauté three or four slices of onion, I hope I do not have to say that you must peel the onion first.

When I speak of putting croutons in an omelette, there is

no rule about the quantity, because that depends on your own taste. Remember, however, that usually they only supplement the other ingredients.

In every recipe it is necessary always to put the ingredients directly into the hot butter before adding the eggs, as I have explained before, so I will not note this fact in each recipe.

In every recipe combining meat with something else, the quantity of meat will be the same. Often the difference between omelettes is only in the combination of ingredients.

With these few cautions, then, let us begin with the various kinds of plain omelettes. Here, of course, you make the PLAIN OMELETTE as I described in the previous chapter and add the ingredients as given in the varieties which follow.

CHEESE OMELETTE (*omelette au fromage*)

This is perhaps the easiest omelette to do because it requires no preparation, except to grate the cheese. I use only Swiss cheese, as I have said, but there is nothing to prevent you from using any kind of cheese you like. For the individual omelette, add 2 tablespoons of grated cheese *to the eggs*. Pour the mixture into the hot butter and finish as for PLAIN OMELETTE.

TOMATO OMELETTE (*omelette aux tomates*)

If you want to peel the tomato (which is not necessary), an easy way to do it is to plunge it into boiling water and then into cold water, after which the skin will come off readily. As soon as the butter is hot in your pan, cut into it 3 to 5 slices of tomato, the number of slices depending on the size. If it is a large tomato, 3 slices are enough. Cook for one minute until the slices are a little browned on one side, then turn them and they will be ready. Salt a little, pour the eggs on top, and finish the omelette.

POTATO OMELETTE (*omelette aux pommes de terre*)

This is Marlene Dietrich's favorite omelette. It is always made with a boiled potato, which may be used cold, but hot is much better. In either case, cut a medium-sized potato into slices, put them in the hot butter, and let them turn a nice golden brown on both sides. Salt a little, then pour the eggs on top and proceed.

ONION OMELETTE (*omelette à l'oignon*)

Take a medium onion, peel it, and cut it into fine slices either across or lengthwise. Sauté the slices in the hot butter rather rapidly—so they will brown and at the same time stay a little crisp. I do not like mushy onions, and I do not think you will. Salt a little, pour the eggs on top, and complete.

LYONNAISE OMELETTE (*omelette Lyonnaise*)

The Lyonnaise omelette is really only another onion omelette, with a slight variation. Fry the onion as described above and add a little chopped parsley. When the omelette is done and is folded onto the plate, pour some brown butter onto the omelette. Brown butter is made by warming 1 tablespoon of butter until it is dark brown, then adding to it ½ teaspoon vinegar. Either wait until butter has cooled before adding vinegar or warm vinegar slightly.

TOASTED BREAD OMELETTE (*omelette aux croûtons*)

Take a piece of French bread one or two days old (preferably the crust); or any hard roll will do. Dice it into about 12 to 15 cubes and fry them in butter until they are golden brown. Pour the eggs on top and complete.

OYSTER PLANT OMELETTE (*omelette aux salsifis*)

This omelette would take a long time to make if you were using fresh oyster plant, and it could be made only in sea-

son (winter); today you can buy this vegetable in a can.
I do not like canned vegetables, but this is different because
it is not a green vegetable and in the can it comes ready
cut in 1-inch or 1½-inch lengths. Cut them again, or dice
them, and dry them well with a towel. Now sauté about
2 or 3 tablespoons of them in butter. Let them come to a
golden brown, salt just a little, and pour the eggs on top
as before to make the omelette.

JERUSALEM ARTICHOKE OMELETTE (*omelette aux topinambours*)

This is a delicious omelette, because it has the taste of
artichokes. Unfortunately people in America do not seem
to like what takes a long time to prepare, and I must tell
you that this vegetable does not come in cans. It must be
peeled, washed, and either cut in slices or diced, until you
have about 2 or 3 tablespoons. Then sauté them slowly in
butter until they are tender, pour the eggs on top, and
complete.

ARTICHOKE HEARTS OMELETTE (*omelette aux coeurs d'artichaux*)

To make this omelette with artichoke hearts, buy frozen
ones unless you can find some tiny artichokes. The frozen
ones are delicious and do not take as long to prepare. Take
2 or 3 of the hearts, depending on their size, and after you
have cooked them according to directions on the package,
cut them in lengthwise strips, or just open the leaves and
sauté them in butter, turning well with a fork. Pour the
eggs on top and complete. When you have fresh artichokes
in season, use only the bottoms and then your dish is called
omelette aux fonds d'artichaux. Prepare and cook one large
artichoke (as you would if you were going to eat it for
its own sake). Discard the leaves, unless you want to eat

them after, *à la vinaigrette*. Cut the bottom in a few pieces and sauté these pieces in butter, turning them with a fork for a minute. Now pour the eggs on top and finish.

GARLIC OMELETTE (*omelette à l'ail*)

Take 2 large or 3 medium cloves of garlic, peel them and cut them in fine slices. When the butter in the pan is hot, put the slices in it and let them take a light color. Pour the eggs on top and complete.

CHIVE OMELETTE (*omelette à la ciboulette*)

When fresh chives are available, in the spring, use them. Just cut them fine (but do not chop them), add to the eggs, then pour the mixture in hot butter and proceed as before. During the rest of the year, when fresh chives are unobtainable, it is perfectly permissible to use frozen ones, but instead of putting them in the eggs, I put them in the butter and turn them a little. However, *don't cook them*. Now pour the eggs on top and complete.

MIXED HERBS OMELETTE (*omelette aux fines herbes*)

This is the favorite of the Duke and Duchess of Windsor. The *fines herbes* consist of parsley, chives, chervil, and tarragon. In the mixture, the parsley should dominate. To approximately 2 tablespoons of chopped parsley add 1 teaspoon of chives, only ¼ teaspoon of chervil, and just a soupçon of tarragon. I sometimes omit the tarragon because it is so strong that it is likely to overwhelm the others. But then I add a little leek, cut fine. Put the herb mixture in the hot butter, shake the pan, pour the eggs on right away, and proceed as before. When sorrel is available in spring, you can add a leaf or two of it (but no tarragon in that case), and you will see how good it is. I prefer putting these *fines herbes* into the butter rather than into the eggs, because it brings out the flavor. But in doing this, a warning: you must be even quicker than usual.

MUSHROOM OMELETTE (*omelette aux champignons*)
Wash and dry 2 or 3 medium-size mushrooms. Slice them and sauté them in butter until they are done, which will take only a minute because mushrooms cook fast. Mix well with a fork. Salt a little, then pour the eggs on top and proceed as before. In France we have many different kinds of mushrooms, which are good for omelettes as well as for a vegetable, but for some reason they do not find favor here, although I have tried to feature them. In my restaurant I tried using cepes, but no one seemed to like them, so I use the only kind available here, the white mushroom that we call in France *champignons de Paris*.

EGGPLANT OMELETTE (*omelette à l'aubergine*)
From a peeled eggplant cut crosswise about 8 pieces the size of a half dollar. Cook them in hot butter until they are done. They cook very quickly. When they are golden brown, salt a little, turning them on both sides, pour the eggs on top, and proceed as before.

SPINACH OMELETTE (*omelette à l'épinard*)
Clean and cook the spinach in boiled salted water. When it is done, squeeze out the water. Chop it a little. Do not purée the spinach unless you prefer it that way. Put it in the pan in hot butter and add a little salt. Turn with a fork. Now pour the eggs on top and complete.

ASPARAGUS OMELETTE (*omelette aux asperges*)
Here again is an omelette which can be made with the fresh vegetable in season, or with the frozen variety, which is a little easier. In either case, the asparagus must be cooked first. Take one large stalk, or two smaller ones, and

cut into small pieces. Put them in hot butter and roll them in it, shaking the pan. Salt a little, put the eggs on top, and proceed as before.

SORREL OR SOURGRASS OMELETTE (*omelette à l'oseille*)

This is a very tasty omelette which has a little tang to it. Take the stems and the ribs of a few leaves of sorrel. A good handful should be enough. Wash them, sponge them, and cut them, but not too fine, or they will shrivel in the cooking. Put them in hot butter, salt a little, and just shake the pan. Pour the eggs on top and proceed. This vegetable is used more often in France than it is here, but when it is nicely prepared it is a very good accompaniment for a roast veal or a leg of lamb.

CAULIFLOWER OMELETTE (*omelette au chou-fleur*)

If you cook an entire cauliflower, you can use it as a vegetable for your meal, but to make the omelette, take only some small flowerets, about 2 tablespoons, and put them in hot butter. Turn them well with a fork until they are golden, salt and pepper a little, then pour the eggs on top and complete.

BACON OMELETTE (*omelette au lard*)

What we in France call *lard*, you call salt pork, and what you call lard is known to us as white fat. By whatever name, it must be not too lean and not too fat, just in between. You may, in fact, use whatever bacon you choose as long as it fits these qualifications. In a separate pan with butter, dice about 10 pieces and cook them a little until they are a golden brown. Do not salt. Now transfer them to the butter in the omelette pan, pour the eggs on top, and complete.

HAM OMELETTE (*omelette au jambon*)

As with the bacon omelette, you can use whatever ham pleases you. Cut about 10 to 12 little pieces and put them in hot butter in the omelette pan. Turn them until they are browned. Do not salt. Pour the eggs on top and complete.

SAUSAGE OMELETTE (*omelette aux saucisses*)

Take 1 or 2 sausages the length and thickness of a finger, dice, and let them cook slowly in the pan without butter. Shake the pan so that they will cook evenly. Then remove all the fat and replace it with butter. Now pour the eggs on top and complete.

CHICKEN OMELETTE (*omelette au poulet*)

Whenever you cook a chicken, keep a piece or two aside to make an omelette. When you make it, dice about 2 or 3 tablespoons. If the chicken is still hot from cooking, just put it in hot butter and pour the eggs on top immediately. If it is cold, you need only warm it up a little in the pan before proceeding.

KIDNEY OMELETTE (*omelette aux rognons de veau*)

Any kind of kidney will do for this one, whichever you prefer. I use veal kidneys myself. Since they are quite large, a half of one should suffice. Cut it in slices, discard the center, and cook the slices slowly in butter in the omelette pan until they are done. Or, if you wish to do it as I do, cook the whole kidney first in a shallow pan, and when it is done, cut half of it in slices. In any case, put the slices in the omelette pan, pour the eggs on top, and complete.

CHICKEN-LIVER OMELETTE (*omelette aux foies de poulet*)

Whenever you cook a chicken, keep the liver to make an

omelette. Livers are, of course, easy to obtain in the butcher shop, if you want more than one omelette. If the liver is a good size, one is enough to cut up for an omelette, or take 2 small ones and cut them in pieces. Sauté them in butter, but not in the omelette pan, because that would make the omelette stick to the bottom. When they are done, salt them a little and transfer them to the omelette pan and the hot butter. Pour the eggs on top immediately and proceed.

GOOSE-LIVER OMELETTE (*omelette au foie gras*)
This one is a little expensive to do every day, especially if you use the real *pâté de foie gras*. If you cannot afford that, it is possible to use the less expensive *purée de foie gras* instead. If you use the real *pâté*, put 1 or 2 tablespoons in the hot butter in the pan—not to cook it, of course, but only to melt it a little. Squash it a bit first, or dice it, put it in the butter, and pour the eggs on top right away and complete. If you are using the *purée*, do the omelette first, and when it is half cooked, add 1 tablespoon or possibly a little more of the *purée*, and proceed.

TRUFFLE OMELETTE (*omelette aux truffes*)
This is also an expensive omelette. When you buy a can of truffles, sometimes there is only one large one, or two or three small ones. One large truffle or two small ones should be enough. I cut them in slices, lengthwise, because I like to see these slices on the omelette. It is much better to do this than to dice them. Don't cook them. Just turn them in the butter once. Before you pour the eggs on top, add to the eggs 1 teaspoon of the juice from the can. Complete the omelette.

CALF'S-BRAIN OMELETTE (*omelette à la cervelle*)
If the brain is small, one is enough, otherwise half of one

should do. After the brain is cooked in boiling salted water, cut it into slices and brown them in the butter. Add a little salt, then the eggs, and complete.

SWEETBREAD OMELETTE (*omelette au riz de veau*)
Follow the same procedure as above. After the sweetbread is parboiled, cut 6 to 8 slices and sauté them in butter, turning them on both sides until they are golden. Salt a little, pour the eggs on top, and complete.

CAVIAR OMELETTE (*omelette au caviar*)
This can be made with either red or black caviar, but the black is much superior. To make it is simplicity itself. Make the omelette, and just before you fold it, add 1 tablespoon of caviar.

WALNUT OMELETTE (*omelette aux noix*)
No reason today to take the trouble to shell walnuts when you can find them already shelled in cans. But if you want to blanch them, soak them for a little while in salted water and the skin should come off without any trouble. It is perfectly permissible to use them just as they come, however. You will need about 2 tablespoons of walnuts for this omelette. Break them in small pieces into the butter, add the eggs, and complete.

CHESTNUT OMELETTE (*omelette aux marrons*)
This omelette also would take a long time to make if you had to cook the chestnuts yourself, but it is easy to find *marrons au naturel* in cans. Break 3 or 4 of them in the hot butter, turn them once or twice, add the eggs, and complete.

APPLE OMELETTE (*omelette aux pommes*)
This omelette really belongs with the sweet ones at the end

of the chapter, but because there is no sugar in it I think it is proper to include it here. Peel and core an apple. Half of it should be enough for the omelette. Cut the half in slices, drop them in hot butter, and cook till they are a golden-brown color on both sides. Do not salt, of course; the salt in the eggs is enough. Now pour the eggs on top and proceed.

Cheese Omelettes

Every omelette in this section requires 1 tablespoon of grated cheese, but you may add more to suit your taste. I use Gruyère but you may use any grated cheese. When bacon is called for, remember that I use salt pork but you may substitute any kind of bacon.

GUIGNOL (onions, cheese) Sauté 1 chopped medium onion until it is golden. Pour in the eggs mixed with 1 tablespoon or more of cheese, and complete.

PARMENTIER (potatoes, cheese) Sauté about 6 slices of boiled potato until they are golden on one side, turn them, salt a little, and pour the eggs mixed with 1 tablespoon of cheese on top.

CHAMBERY (potatoes, onions, cheese) Sauté 3 slices of onion, and when they are half done, add 3 or 4 slices of boiled potato. Let the potato cook until it is a golden color, then turn, salt a little, and mix well with a fork as you shake the pan. Now pour the eggs on top and proceed.

LAURENTIENNE (*fines herbes*, cheese) Toss into the butter 1 good tablespoon of *fines herbes*, quickly pour the eggs mixed with the cheese on top, then complete.

MARIA (onions, *fines herbes*, cheese) Sauté 3 slices of

onion. When they are browned, add 1 tablespoon of *fines herbes*, pour the egg mixed with the cheese on top, and finish the omelette.

DAUPHINOISE (potatoes in CREAM SAUCE, cheese) Sauté 3 or 4 slices of boiled potato until golden, add CREAM SAUCE, then pour the eggs mixed with the cheese on top and complete. If you do not want to bother to make the CREAM SAUCE, just add 1 tablespoon of cream when the potatoes are golden.

VALENCIENNES (onions, peas, croutons, cheese) Sauté 3 slices of onion, and when they are half done, add 4 or 5 croutons. Toss this all together and add 1 tablespoon of cooked peas (canned peas will also do). Mix well again, pour the eggs mixed with the cheese on top, and complete.

ARLEGEOISE (onions, spinach, rice, cheese) Sauté 3 slices of onion. When they are golden, add 1 tablespoon of cooked and chopped spinach and 1 tablespoon of cooked rice. Mix well with a fork, salt a little, pour in the eggs mixed with cheese, and complete as usual.

CHOISY (peas, onions, rice, parsley, cheese) Sauté 3 slices of onions until done. Add 1 tablespoon of cooked peas and 1 tablespoon of cooked rice. Mix well. Add 1 teaspoon of chopped parsley. Pour in the eggs mixed with the cheese and complete.

ARGENTEUIL (asparagus, parsley, cheese) Use 2 stalks of cooked asparagus cut in small pieces, and shake the pan so they will roll evenly in the butter. Sprinkle a little parsley over the eggs mixed with the cheese, and complete.

FONTAINEBLEAU (eggplant, garlic, *fines herbes*, cheese, TOMATO SAUCE) Sauté 6 to 8 slices of eggplant. When they are done on both sides, add a little garlic, sprinkle with *fines herbes* or parsley and a little salt. Pour in the eggs mixed with cheese, and complete. Top with 2 tablespoons of TOMATO SAUCE.

MORNAY (tomatoes, croutons, *fines herbes*, cheese) Sauté 3 slices of tomato (not too thin or they will shrink, but not too thick either). When they are browned, turn them on the other side and add 4 or 5 croutons, and 1 teaspoon of *fines herbes*, and a little salt. Pour in the eggs mixed with cheese, and complete.

BRESSANE (croutons, CREAM SAUCE, cheese) Into the pan with the hot butter put 12 to 15 croutons made with the crust of French bread or a hard roll. When they are golden, add CREAM SAUCE and pour the eggs mixed with cheese over them. If you don't want to make the CREAM SAUCE, add 1 tablespoon of cream before putting in the eggs.

LORRAINE (chives, bacon, *fines herbes*, cheese) Sauté 5 or 6 pieces of diced bacon, then add 1 tablespoon of chives and 1 teaspoon of *fines herbes* or parsley. Pour in the eggs mixed with cheese, and complete.

LIMOUSINE (potatoes, bacon, *fines herbes*, cheese) First sauté 5 or 6 cubes of bacon and put them aside. Then cut about 5 slices of boiled potato and sauté them until golden. Turn them on the other side and add the bacon, 1 teaspoon of *fines herbes* or parsley, and pour in the eggs mixed with cheese and proceed.

BEAUVILLIER (bacon, croutons, olive, cheese) You can do the bacon and croutons together, but put in the bacon first, 6 to 8 cubes, and when they are half done, add 5 or 6 croutons. Toss well together, pour in the eggs mixed with cheese, add 1 olive cut in pieces, and complete.

FRANCHE-COMTOISE (asparagus tips, bacon, parsley, cheese) Do the bacon first, 6 to 8 cubes. When they are half done, add 2 stalks of cooked and cut asparagus. Sprinkle with 1 teaspoon of parsley and toss in the pan. Shake it, pour in the eggs mixed with cheese, and complete.

DAUPHIN (bacon, spinach, croutons, cheese) Proceed as for the BEAUVILLIER, above, but add 1 tablespoon of cooked and chopped spinach. Mix well with a fork, pour in the eggs mixed with cheese, and proceed.

ROCHAMBEAU (sausage, spinach, mushrooms, cheese) Sauté 1 medium sliced mushroom and 1 sausage cut in pieces. Shake the pan well. When the mixture is done, add 1 tablespoon of cooked and chopped spinach. Mix well, pour in the eggs mixed with cheese, and complete.

BAMBOCHE (chicory, croutons, bacon, garlic, cheese) Prepare like the DAUPHIN, above, but substitute chicory for spinach, prepared the same way. Add garlic and proceed.

DUMONTEIL (carrots, onions, bacon, *fines herbes*, cheese) Sauté 3 slices of onion with 5 or 6 cubes of bacon in the omelette pan. When they are browned, add 1 or 2 boiled carrots, sliced. Mix well with a fork. Sprinkle with *fines herbes* or parsley, then pour in the eggs mixed with cheese and proceed.

CHAMPENOISE (oyster plant, rice, parsley, CREAM SAUCE, cheese) Proceed exactly as for OYSTER PLANT OMELETTE, but add 1 tablespoon of cooked rice, and 1 tablespoon of CREAM SAUCE to the oyster plant. Mix well, then pour in the eggs mixed with cheese, and complete.

AURILLAC (oyster plant, bacon, croutons, noodles, cheese) Sauté 5 or 6 pieces of diced bacon, 5 or 6 croutons, and 1 tablespoon of diced cooked oyster plant all together. When the mixture has browned, add 1 tablespoon of cooked noodles. Turn with a fork, pour in the eggs mixed with cheese, and complete.

MONTPELLIER (cauliflower in CREAM SAUCE, croutons, cheese) Make a CREAM SAUCE as described in the section on sauces. Cut into it some flowerets from a cooked cauliflower. In the omelette pan, sauté in butter about 8 croutons. When they are golden, add the flowerets taken out of the CREAM SAUCE, leaving just a little of the CREAM SAUCE on them. Mix with a fork, pour in the eggs mixed with cheese, and finish.

COLMAR (cauliflower, bacon, croutons, cheese) Sauté the bacon and croutons together, about 5 or 6 pieces of each. When they are brown, add some flowerets of cooked cauliflower, about 8 to 10 pieces. Mix well together, pour in the eggs mixed with cheese, and finish.

FANTASIO (apples, croutons, walnuts, cheese) Peel an apple. Cut half of it in slices, and sauté them in butter with 6 or 8 croutons. When they are done on one side, turn on the other and add to the mixture 1 or 2 walnuts. Now pour in the eggs mixed with cheese and complete.

MARGOT (truffles and cheese) Cut a whole truffle in slices and put them into the hot butter. Turn them just once, then pour in the eggs mixed with cheese, adding 1 teaspoon of juice from the truffle can, and complete as before.

Tomato Omelettes

(OMELETTES AUX TOMATES)

In these omelettes, the number of tomato slices will depend on the size of the tomato. I always use a medium-size one.

CREOLE (tomatoes, onions) Sauté 3 or 4 slices of onion. When they are half done, cut in 3 slices of tomato and let them cook together, turning the tomatoes. Add salt and pepper to taste, pour in the eggs and complete.

NIMOISE (tomatoes, onions, green pepper) Sauté 3 or 4 slices of onion, and cut into it 8 or 10 pieces of green pepper. Cook together slowly, until the peppers are soft, then add 2 slices of tomato. Finish cooking, salt and pepper to taste, then pour in the eggs and complete.

NICOISE (tomatoes, olives, garlic, parsley) In Nice this omelette is made with Swiss chard, tomatoes, and eggplant, but I have simplified it by making it with tomatoes and olives only. Sauté about 4 or 5 slices of tomato. Cook them until they are browned on one side, and turn them over. Salt and pepper to taste, then add a little garlic and some chopped parsley. Cut an olive or two into the eggs, then pour in the eggs and complete.

MIREILLE (tomatoes, onions, croutons, parsley) Make as for the CREOLE, but add croutons.

MARIANNE (tomatoes, *fines herbes*, cheese)   Make as for the NICOISE; add *fines herbes* or parsley. Put 1 tablespoon grated cheese in the eggs, then pour in the eggs and complete.

ARLESIENNE (tomatoes, summer squash, onions, garlic, parsley)   You can put the three vegetables together if you cook them slowly. Let them brown a little, add a little garlic, salt, and pepper, sprinkle with parsley, pour in the eggs, and complete.

MISTRAL (tomatoes, eggplant, garlic, *fines herbes*)   Made like the ARLESIENNE.

PROVENCALE (tomatoes, mushrooms, garlic, *fines herbes*)   Again, like the ARLESIENNE.

TOSCA (tomatoes, potatoes, garlic, *fines herbes*)   Sauté 3 or 4 slices of boiled potato in butter until they are golden, turn them over, and add 2 slices of tomato. Cook together, add a little garlic, sprinkle with *fines herbes*, pour on the eggs, and complete.

CHATILLON (tomatoes, noodles, olives, *fines herbes*)   The noodles have to be cooked beforehand. Sauté 3 slices of tomato, then add about 2 tablespoons of the cooked noodles. Salt and pepper to taste. Sprinkle *fines herbes* or parsley on top, cut 1 medium olive into the eggs, and proceed.

NEUFCHATEL (tomatoes, noodles, peas, onions)   Made like the CHATILLON, above, but add 1 tablespoon of cooked or canned peas.

CHARBONNIERE (tomatoes, mushrooms, onions, croutons)   Made like the CHATILLON, above.

MATIGNON (tomatoes, green pepper, rice, olives, garlic)
Use 2 or 3 slices of tomato and 6 or 8 pieces of diced green
pepper, cooked together. Add 1 tablespoon of cooked rice
and a little garlic. Into the eggs or the pan cut 1 or 2 olives.
Pour on the eggs and complete.

ANTIBOISE (tomatoes, eggplant, summer squash, garlic,
parsley) Made like the MISTRAL, but adding 2 or 3 slices
of summer squash.

ALGERIENNE (tomatoes, pimientos, green pepper, rice,
basil, parsley) Use 3 slices of tomato, 6 or 8 slices of diced
green pepper, and 5 or 6 pieces of diced pimiento. Cook all
these together, then add 1 tablespoon of cooked rice, a
soupçon of basil, and 1 teaspoon of parsley. Mix all of it
well, then pour on the eggs and complete.

MONTBRISON (tomatoes, spinach, croutons, garlic)
Sauté 3 slices of tomato, add 5 or 6 croutons, 1 tablespoon
of cooked spinach, and a little garlic. Pour on the eggs and
complete.

JOINVILLE (tomatoes, spinach, onions, rice, parsley) Use
2 slices of onion and 2 slices of tomato, cooked together.
When they are done, add 1 tablespoon of cooked spinach
and 1 tablespoon of cooked rice. Mix all this well, sprinkle
with parsley, add eggs, and complete.

AVIGNON (tomatoes, mushrooms, spinach, noodles, croutons) Sauté 2 slices of tomato and 5 or 6 slices of mushroom. Add 1 tablespoon of cooked spinach, 1 tablespoon
of cooked noodles, and 5 or 6 croutons. Mix well with a
fork, add eggs, and complete.

BASQUE, also called PIPERADE (tomatoes, green pepper,
onions, garlic, bacon) Stew 3 slices of tomato together

with 6 or 8 pieces of diced green pepper, 3 slices of onion, and a little garlic. Do the bacon in another pan, 5 or 6 cubes of it, and add it when everything else is cooked. Combine all thoroughly, add eggs, and complete.

MONEGASQUE (tomatoes, asparagus, peas, croutons) Sauté 2 slices of tomato, add 1 stalk of cooked asparagus cut into pieces, 1 tablespoon of cooked peas, and 4 or 5 croutons. Pour in the eggs and complete.

ANDALOUSE (tomatoes, eggplant, bacon, noodles, garlic) In the omelette pan cook together 3 slices of tomato and 4 or 5 pieces of eggplant. Sauté the bacon in another pan, then add it with some cooked noodles and a little garlic to the tomato mixture. Add the eggs and complete.

MONTREUIL (tomatoes, eggplant, rice, bacon, parsley) Prepare like the ANDALOUSE, above.

BOULOGNE (tomatoes, mushrooms, bacon, croutons) Cook the bacon and croutons separately. Into the omelette pan cut 3 slices of tomato with 6 or 8 slices of mushroom. When they are done, combine all ingredients thoroughly, and complete omelette.

COURS VERDUN (tomatoes, potatoes, bacon, onions, cheese) Sauté 3 slices of onion with 3 slices of boiled potato. Add 2 slices of tomato and 5 or 6 cubes of fried bacon. Mix everything together well, then pour in the eggs with cheese and complete.

Vegetable Omelettes

JARDINIERE (carrots, peas, asparagus, tomatoes) Into your pan, when the butter is hot, cut 2 slices of tomato. When they are done on one side, turn them. Now add 1 stalk of cooked asparagus cut into pieces, and a few slices of boiled carrot. Add 1 tablespoon of cooked peas. Mix all this well with a fork and shake the pan. Add salt. Now pour the eggs on top and complete.

CRECY (carrots, rice, *fines herbes*, cheese) If you have time, you can cook 1 raw carrot sliced finely into the butter, and done slowly. If you do not, cut a boiled carrot into slices (2 carrots if they are small), put these slices into the butter, and let them brown a little. I always use only young, small carrots. Add 1 tablespoon of cooked rice and 1 teaspoon of *fines herbes* or parsley. Pour in the eggs mixed with 1 tablespoon grated cheese, add salt, and complete.

GAULOISE (potatoes, onions, leeks, *fines herbes*) Fry 3 or 4 slices of onion in butter for a minute. Cut into the pan 4 or 5 slices of boiled potato, turning them on both sides. Add a little leek and 1 teaspoon of *fines herbes* or parsley. Salt to taste, pour in the eggs, and complete.

SAVOYARDE (potatoes, garlic, CREAM SAUCE, *fines herbes*) Sauté about 5 slices of boiled potato. When they are pale golden on one side, turn them over. Do not brown them. Add salt and a hint of garlic, also 1 teaspoon *fines herbes* or parsley. Add the CREAM SAUCE, and pour on the eggs right away. If you do not want to bother making the CREAM SAUCE, you can add 1 tablespoon of cream. Finish as usual.

VALFLEURY (spinach, croutons, rice, garlic) Fry the croutons first, about 5 to 8 of them, then add 2 tablespoons of cooked spinach and 1 tablespoon of cooked rice, with a hint of garlic. Mix well with a fork, then pour in the eggs and complete.

VILLAGEOISE (mushrooms, noodles, croutons, garlic, olives, herbs) Sauté 1 medium-size mushroom, sliced, with 4 or 5 croutons. Add 1 tablespoon of cooked noodles, a hint of garlic, and sprinkle with herbs or parsley. Now pour the eggs on top and cut an olive in slivers into the pan. Proceed as usual.

CLAMART (peas, onions, croutons, lettuce, CREAM SAUCE) Fry 3 or 4 slices of onion, add 4 or 5 croutons, 2 tablespoons of cooked peas, and 1 or 2 lettuce leaves cut into the pan. Add 1 tablespoon of CREAM SAUCE. Mix all well, then pour the eggs on top and complete.

MADELON (eggplant, onions, rice, *fines herbes*, TOMATO SAUCE) Start with 2 slices of onion in the pan. When they are half done, add 4 or 5 slices of eggplant and 1 tablespoon of cooked rice. Finish cooking. Mix it all well with a fork, add salt, then pour the eggs on top and proceed as usual. When the omelette is folded, pour on 2 or 3 tablespoons of warmed TOMATO SAUCE.

COLBERT (eggplant, summer squash, carrots, garlic, parsley) Sauté together in the pan 3 or 4 slices each of eggplant, summer squash, and boiled carrot. Let these cook a little, shaking the pan and turning them when they are done on one side. Add salt and just a little garlic. Sprinkle with parsley, pour the eggs on top, and finish as usual.

FLORENTINE (spinach, mushrooms, croutons, garlic)

Sauté 1 medium-size mushroom, sliced, and add 4 or 5 croutons. When this is done, add 1 tablespoon or more of cooked, chopped spinach, and a little garlic. Salt to taste and mix well. Now pour the eggs on top and complete.

MONTARGIS (artichoke hearts, garlic, cheese) Take 2 or 3 artichoke hearts and break them into the butter. Shake the pan so that they will absorb the butter, and add a little garlic. Put 1 tablespoon of grated cheese into the eggs and proceed as usual.

CARNOT (asparagus tips, mushrooms, peas, croutons, parsley) Sauté 1 medium-size mushroom, sliced, with 4 or 5 croutons. Add 1 stalk of cooked asparagus cut in pieces, and 1 tablespoon of cooked peas. Shake the pan well and mix with a fork. Add salt and sprinkle with parsley. Then pour the eggs on top and complete.

MOISSONNEUR (potatoes, spinach, bacon, onions) Sauté 3 slices of onion with 3 slices of boiled potato. When this is done, add 5 or 6 little lardons (cubes of salt pork or bacon), done separately, and 1 tablespoon of cooked spinach. Mix all of this thoroughly in the pan, and shake it. Then pour the eggs on top and proceed.

ST. AUBER (artichoke hearts, asparagus, croutons, garlic) Break 2 artichoke hearts and sauté in butter, with 1 stalk of cooked asparagus, sliced. Add 4 or 5 croutons ánd a little garlic. Mix well, pour in the eggs, and finish.

COLETTE (asparagus tips, lardons, croutons, parsley) Cook the lardons in a separate pan. Then cut 2 stalks of cooked asparagus into the omelette pan. Now add 4 or 5 croutons. Shake the pan well and add the lardons. Sprinkle with parsley, then pour in the eggs and complete.

PONT NEUF (potatoes, lardons, spinach, garlic) Follow the MOISSONNEUR recipe. Do the lardons separately, 4 or 5 of them. Use 3 or 4 slices of boiled potato, 1 tablespoon of cooked spinach, and a hint of garlic.

HONFLEUR (green pepper, onions, rice, croutons, parsley, TOMATO SAUCE)   Sauté 2 or 3 slices of onion with 6 or 8 cubes of green pepper. Add 4 or 5 croutons. Mix all this well with a fork. Salt to taste and sprinkle with parsley. When the omelette is folded, cover with 2 or 3 tablespoons of warmed TOMATO SAUCE.

LE VESINET (eggplant, peppers, onions, rice, parsley, TO-MATO SAUCE)   Same as above, only add 2 or 3 pieces of eggplant.

LA FEUILLEE (tomatoes, spinach, onions, rice, parsley) Sauté 2 slices of tomato with 2 slices of onion, mixing with a fork and turning the tomatoes. Add 1 tablespoon of chopped and cooked spinach, also 1 tablespoon of rice. Sprinkle with parsley, shake the pan, pour on the eggs, and complete.

CORDELIERS (artichoke hearts, peas, croutons, truffles, CREAM SAUCE)   Break 2 or 3 artichoke hearts into the pan, add 1 tablespoon of peas and 4 or 5 croutons. Mix well in the pan. Now cut into it 1 slice of truffle and add 1 tablespoon of CREAM SAUCE or cream. Pour in the eggs and proceed.

MULATIERE (asparagus, peas, noodles, truffles, CREAM SAUCE)   Sauté 1 or 2 stalks of cooked asparagus in the butter, with 1 tablespoon of cooked peas and the same amount of cooked noodles. Mix well. Now cut into it 1 slice of truffle and add 1 tablespoon of CREAM SAUCE or cream. Pour in the eggs and complete.

LAFAYETTE (mushrooms, tomatoes, noodles, truffles) Sauté 5 or 6 slices of mushroom together with 2 slices of tomato cut a little thick. Salt to taste. Turn the slices over. Now add 1 or 2 tablespoons of cooked noodles and 1 slice of truffle. Mix well, pour in the eggs, and complete.

French Bacon Omelettes

(OMELETTES AU LARD)

I have already explained that, in French cooking, *lard* is salt pork, but let me repeat that you may use whatever kind of bacon you choose in making these omelettes. Lardons are little cubes of bacon. Be sure that you salt very lightly, because the salt in the bacon will be almost enough. And cook your bacon in a separate pan. For each of these omelettes, 6 to 8 cubes of bacon are enough.

PAYSANNE (French bacon, potatoes) In the omelette pan, sauté 6 or 8 slices of a boiled potato. When they are browned on one side, turn them over. Now add the bacon, 6 or 8 cubes. Shake the pan, then pour in the eggs and proceed.

GRAND'MERE (French bacon, croutons, *fines herbes*) Cook the lardons separately. In the omelette pan sauté about 8 to 10 little croutons. When they are golden, add the lardons and 1 teaspoon of *fines herbes*. Then pour in the eggs and proceed.

PONCET (French bacon, potatoes, *fines herbes*) Sauté 5 or 6 slices of a boiled potato. When they are done, turn them and add the bacon from the other pan. Shake the omelette pan, add 1 teaspoon of *fines herbes*, then pour in the eggs.

MANON (French bacon, mushrooms, rice, *fines herbes*)
Sauté 1 medium-size mushroom, sliced. When it is done,
add the bacon, 1 tablespoon of cooked rice, and 1 teaspoon of *fines herbes*. Pour in the eggs.

VOLNAY (French bacon, potatoes, spinach, garlic, *fines
herbes*) Sauté 4 or 5 slices of boiled potato, add 1 tablespoon of cooked spinach, then the bacon, 1 teaspoon of
fines herbes, and a little garlic. Pour in the eggs.

Now that you know the procedures, I will give you briefly
some variations on the bacon omelette, in which I have listed
the quantity of ingredients where it is necessary. Where the
amount is not given, simply refer to the recipes above where
the ingredient was used, and the amount will be the same.

SOUBISE (French bacon, onions, rice, *fines herbes*, TOMATO
SAUCE) Three slices of onion, 1 tablespoon of cooked rice,
2 or 3 tablespoons of TOMATO SAUCE.

VOLTAIRE (French bacon, mushrooms, croutons, onions,
fines herbes) 3 slices of onion, 1 medium-size mushroom,
sliced, 5 or 6 croutons.

MONSELET (French bacon, artichoke hearts, garlic, rice)
Break 2 or 3 artichoke hearts into the pan, shake the pan,
add a little garlic, and 1 tablespoon of cooked rice.

MASSENET (French bacon, asparagus tips, peas, noodles,
parsley) Cut 2 stalks of asparagus, add 1 tablespoon of
peas, and 1 tablespoon of noodles.

VILLEROY (French bacon, artichoke hearts, peas, croutons) 2 artichoke hearts, 1 tablespoon of peas, 5 or 6 croutons.

BARIGOULE (French bacon, artichoke hearts, mushrooms, garlic) 1 medium-size mushroom, 2 artichoke hearts.

BOULANGERE (French bacon, potatoes, onions, cheese) 3 slices of onion, 5 or 6 slices of boiled potato, and don't forget to put the grated cheese in the eggs.

LAMBALLE (French bacon, peas, mushrooms, croutons, garlic, cheese)

MASSENA (French bacon, artichoke hearts, asparagus tips, rice)

ORLEANS (French bacon, eggplant, green pepper, rice, garlic, TOMATO SAUCE) Start the 5 or 6 cubes of green pepper a little before the eggplant, of which you will need 4 or 5 pieces. Then cook together. Pour TOMATO SAUCE on top of folded omelette.

MARIGNAN (French bacon, spinach, mushrooms, noodles, CREAM SAUCE)

CHENONCEAUX (French bacon, peppers, mushrooms, rice, garlic, TOMATO SAUCE)

FAUBONNE (French bacon, peas, onions, croutons, CREAM SAUCE)

LANGEAIS (French bacon, asparagus, croutons, noodles, *fines herbes*)

CLUNY (French bacon, tomatoes, eggplant, garlic, *fines herbes*)

POULBOT (French bacon, mushrooms, spinach, rice, croutons)

VAUBECOUR (French bacon, tomatoes, mushrooms, noodles, *fines herbes*)

FREJUS (French bacon, peppers, onions, croutons, TOMATO SAUCE)

FLEURIEU (French bacon, ham, tomatoes, summer squash, garlic, parsley)

VAUCLUSE (French bacon, ham, potatoes, spinach, cheese)

HEYRIEUX (French bacon, mushrooms, spinach, rice, truffles, CREAM SAUCE)

TOURNON (French bacon, oyster plant, *fine herbes*, cheese)

PLACE CARNOT (French bacon, mushrooms, truffles, rice, croutons, herbs)

BUTTES-CHAUMONT (French bacon, potatoes, chicory, CREAM SAUCE, cheese)

Chicken-Liver Omelettes

(OMELETTES AUX FOIES DE POULET)

In all these omelettes, it is better to sauté the chicken livers in a separate pan. The quantity in each of them is 1 chicken liver, unless they are very small; then use 2. Cut into cubes.

MAISON (chicken liver, rice, mushrooms)   In the omelette pan sauté 1 medium-size sliced mushroom. When it is done, add 1 tablespoon of cooked rice, then the chicken liver. Salt to taste, add the eggs, and complete.

CHASSEUR (chicken liver, mushrooms, garlic, *fines herbes*) Sauté 1 large mushroom, sliced. When it is done, add a little garlic, then the liver. Salt to taste and add 1 teaspoon of *fines herbes* or parsley. Pour on the eggs and complete.

PRINCESSE (chicken liver, mushrooms, artichoke hearts) Sauté 1 medium-size sliced mushroom and 1 artichoke heart, broken in pieces. Add the liver. Mix well. Salt to taste, add the eggs, and complete.

LILY PONS (chicken liver, tomatoes, mushrooms, olives, parsley) Sauté 1 medium-size sliced mushroom and 2 slices of tomato. When they are done, add the liver. Mix all well. Cut into it 1 olive. Sprinkle with parsley. Pour on the eggs and finish.

FINANCIERE (chicken liver, ham, bacon, mushrooms, truffles, sherry)   Sauté 1 sliced mushroom with 4 or 5 cubes of ham and 4 or 5 lardons. Add the liver and 2 slices of truffle. Sprinkle with sherry, then complete.

REGENCE (chicken liver, tomatoes, rice, garlic, *fines herbes*)   Sauté 3 slices of tomato. When they are done on one side, turn them and add 1 tablespoon of cooked rice. Salt to taste. Now add the liver and a little garlic. Sprinkle with *fines herbes*, turn well with a fork, add eggs, and complete.

MEDICI (chicken liver, peas, rice, onions, croutons)   Sauté 3 slices of onion and 4 to 5 croutons. When they are done, add 1 tablespoon of cooked peas and 1 tablespoon of cooked rice. Salt to taste. Add the liver, mix well, add the eggs, and complete.

REJANE (chicken liver, eggplant, lardons, garlic, parsley) Sauté 5 or 6 pieces or slices of eggplant, and add some lardons, 4 or 5. Now add the liver, a little garlic, and sprinkle with parsley. Salt to taste. Pour on the eggs and complete.

Now I will give you some variations on chicken-liver omelettes. I have listed only the ingredients, except where it is necessary to indicate a quantity. Otherwise, follow the amounts and procedures given above.

CYRANO (chicken liver, lardons, spinach, rice)   1 tablespoon of cooked spinach, 1 tablespoon of cooked rice, 4 or 5 lardons.

RECAMIER (chicken liver, mushrooms, onions, olives)   3 slices of onion, 1 medium-size mushroom, 1 olive.

BOVARY (chicken liver, rice, onions, croutons, olives, *fines herbes*)

LAVOISIER (chicken liver, noodles, mushrooms, garlic)

CRILLON (chicken liver, peas, croutons, CREAM SAUCE, parsley)

MARIE STUART (chicken liver, rice, peas, lardons, croutons)

GEORGE SAND (chicken liver, eggplant, tomatoes, garlic, *fines herbes*)

MADAME DE SEVIGNE (chicken liver, spinach, onions, croutons)

PRADO (chicken liver, lardons, artichoke hearts, rice, garlic)

PORTE DAUPHINE (chicken liver, eggplant, peppers, rice, TOMATO SAUCE)

VERT GALANT (chicken liver, asparagus, peas, croutons, garlic, cheese)

LAPEROUSE (chicken liver, spinach, bacon, croutons, garlic, cheese)

BAUDETTE (chicken liver, mushrooms, spinach, rice, cheese)

ROHANS (chicken liver, bacon, potatoes, garlic, parsley, cheese)

AIGLON (chicken liver, mushrooms, truffles, sherry)

ROXANE (chicken liver, lardons, noodles, mushrooms, truffles, sherry)

LA COLISEE (chicken liver, artichoke hearts, *foie gras*, truffles, cheese, sherry)

GRAND VATEL (chicken liver, mushrooms, walnuts, truffles, cheese, sherry)

PRUNIER (chicken liver, tomato, spinach, mushrooms, *foie gras*, croutons, cheese)

LES ACACIAS (chicken liver, ham, *foie gras*, tomatoes, croutons, Courvoisier)

Veal-Kidney Omelettes

(OMELETTES AUX ROGNONS DE VEAU)

I make these omelettes with veal kidney, but if your prefer some other kind of kidney, it will make no difference. If you do not trust yourself to cook the kidney with the ingredients, do it in a separate pan and then add it to the other ingredients in your omelette pan.

AIX LES BAINS (kidney, ham, tomatoes, olives, *fines herbes*) Start the kidney first. Sauté in the butter 5 or 6 slices of kidney, also 3 or 4 cubes of ham, and 2 slices of tomato. Cook together, turning the kidney and the tomato. Salt to taste. Shake the pan. Cut into it 1 olive. Sprinkle some *fines herbes* or parsley, add the eggs, and complete.

VERSAILLES (kidney, lardons, tomatoes, rice, peas, parsley) Start the kidney first. Sauté 5 or 6 slices of kidney and 2 slices of tomato. Let them cook together nicely, turning with the fork. Salt to taste. Add 1 tablespoon of cooked rice and 1 tablespoon of cooked peas. Shake the pan. Add the lardons, sprinkle with parsley, pour on the eggs, and complete.

TREVOUX (kidney, ham, mushrooms, spinach) Sauté 5 or 6 slices of kidney, 4 or 5 cubes of ham, and 1 medium-size mushroom, sliced. When they are done, add 1 tablespoon of cooked spinach. Salt to taste. Mix well, add the eggs, and complete.

AMBASSADEUR (kidney, lardons, croutons, olives, MA- DEIRA SAUCE) You will need a little more kidney here, 6 or 8 slices. Add to it 4 or 5 lardons and 4 or 5 croutons. When the kidney is done on one side, turn it over. Cut into it 1 olive. Mix well, pour on the eggs, and complete. When the omelette has been folded, cover it with the MADEIRA SAUCE, about 3 tablespoons.

MARECHALE (kidney, mushrooms, artichoke hearts, rice, SHERRY SAUCE) Sauté 1 medium-size mushroom, sliced, with 1 or 2 artichoke hearts, broken. When they are done, add 1 tablespoon of cooked rice, 5 or 6 slices of kidney, pre- viously sautéed. Salt to taste. Mix well and pour on the eggs. When it is done, cover it with the sauce.

IMPERIALE (kidney, artichoke hearts, croutons, MADEIRA SAUCE) Sauté 5 slices of kidney with 2 broken artichoke hearts. Salt and pepper to taste. When they are nicely cooked, add 4 or 5 croutons. Mix well and pour on the eggs. Cover with the sauce when done.

BEAUHARNAIS (kidney, tomatoes, mushrooms, noodles, garlic, *fines herbes*) Sauté 5 or 6 slices of kidney. When they are half done, add 1 small mushroom, sliced, and 2 slices of tomato. Salt and pepper to taste. Cook together. Add 1 tablespoon of cooked noodles and a little garlic. Sprinkle with *fines herbes* or parsley. Mix well, pour on the eggs, and finish.

MARCEAU (kidney, mushrooms, peas, rice, croutons, *fines herbes*) Sauté 5 or 6 slices of kidney and 1 medium-size sliced mushroom. When they are cooked, add 1 tablespoon of cooked peas, 1 tablespoon of cooked rice, 4 or 5 croutons, and sprinkle with herbs. Mix well, pour on the eggs, and complete.

NAPOLEON (kidney, ham, eggplant, croutons, garlic, *fines herbes*) Sauté 5 or 6 slices of kidney. When they are half done, add 4 or 5 sliced pieces of eggplant, 3 or 4 cubes of ham, and 4 or 5 croutons. Cook together, add a little garlic, herbs, salt and pepper to taste. Pour on the eggs and complete.

TAVERNIER (kidney, eggplant, onions, green pepper, *fines herbes*, TOMATO SAUCE) For this one you should definitely cook the kidney in another pan. Into the omelette pan cut 3 slices of onion, 4 or 5 slices of eggplant, and 5 or 6 cubes of green pepper. Sauté, shaking the pan frequently. Salt and pepper to taste. Add the kidney and mix well. Sprinkle with *fines herbes* or parsley. When the omelette is folded, cover with the TOMATO SAUCE.

PONT TILSITT (kidney, ham, mushrooms, noodles, *fines herbes*, TOMATO SAUCE) Begin with the kidney, 5 or 6 slices. When they are half done, add 1 mushroom, sliced, and 4 or 5 cubes of ham. Finish cooking. Add 1 tablespoon of cooked noodles, and mix again. Add the *fines herbes* and the eggs and complete the omelette. When it is folded, cover with TOMATO SAUCE.

GERARD PHILIPPE (kidney, lardons, croutons, rice, olives, SHERRY SAUCE) Cook the lardons separately. In the omelette pan sauté the kidney slices. When they are done on both sides, add 4 or 5 croutons, the lardons, and 1 tablespoon of cooked rice. Mix well together, add the eggs, into which you have sliced 1 olive, and complete. When folded, cover with SHERRY SAUCE.

Now here are the variations. I have listed only the ingredients, except where it is necessary to indicate a quantity. Otherwise, follow the amounts and procedures given above.

TALLEYRAND (kidney, mushrooms, spinach, rice, MA-DEIRA SAUCE)

DE CASTELLANE (kidney, asparagus tips, rice, mush-rooms, SHERRY SAUCE) 1 medium-size mushroom, 1 stalk of asparagus, 1 tablespoon of cooked rice.

PLACE LE VISTE (kidney, potatoes, lardons, spinach, cheese) 4 or 5 slices of potato, 4 or 5 lardons, 1 table-spoon of cooked spinach, 1 tablespoon of grated cheese in the eggs.

COURS EUGENIE (kidney, bacon, tomatoes, oyster plant, SHERRY SAUCE) 2 slices of tomato, 6 to 8 cubes of oyster plant, 4 or 5 cubes of bacon.

JEAN DE TOURNES (kidney, ham, onions, mushrooms, rice, MADEIRA SAUCE)

BOUGIVAL (kidney, ham, mushrooms, peppers, garlic, TO-MATO SAUCE)

DE VALVERT (kidney, bacon, artichoke hearts, rice, MA-DEIRA SAUCE)

BOILEAU (kidney, ham, bacon, eggplant, rice, herbs, TO-MATO SAUCE)

SEBASTOPOL (kidney, mushrooms, onions, bacon, SHERRY SAUCE)

SOLFERINO (kidney, mushrooms, croutons, truffles, SAUCE VELOUTE)

PALAIS GRILLET (kidney, *foie gras*, tomatoes, truffles, SHERRY SAUCE)

PALAIS RAMEAU (kidney, *foie gras*, spinach, croutons, walnuts, sherry)

CELESTINS (kidney, mushrooms, truffles, cheese, MADEIRA SAUCE)

JEAN VALLIER (kidney, *foie gras*, ham, truffles, artichoke hearts, SAUCE VELOUTE)

RIVOLI (kidney, *foie gras*, mushrooms, spinach, croutons, MADEIRA SAUCE)

SEDAN (kidney, *foie gras*, mushrooms, walnuts, cheese)

Mushroom Omelettes

(OMELETTES AUX CHAMPIGNONS)

VAL D'ISERE (mushrooms, cheese)   Sauté 1 large or 2 medium-size mushrooms. When nicely done, salt to taste. Pour in the eggs, to which has been added 1 tablespoon of grated cheese.

FLORENT (mushrooms, asparagus)   1 medium-size mushroom, sliced, and 1 stalk of cooked asparagus, cut in small pieces. Sauté these together, salt to taste, and complete.

BRETONNE (mushrooms, onions, leeks, *fines herbes*)   Sauté 3 or 4 slices of onion, also 1 medium-size sliced mushroom. When they are done, add 2 or 3 slices of the bottom of a leek, or cut a little of the green from the center. Add 1 teaspoon of *fines herbes* or parsley. Salt to taste and proceed.

BUCHERONNE (mushrooms, onion, cheese, parsley)   Make like the BRETONNE, above, adding grated cheese to the eggs.

MARENGO (mushrooms, croutons, garlic, TOMATO SAUCE)   Sauté 1 large or 2 medium-size sliced mushrooms with 6 to 8 croutons. The croutons should be added only when the mushrooms are done, because it does not take long for them to cook. Add a little garlic and a little salt. When the omelette has been folded, pour on the TOMATO SAUCE.

DE VIGNY (mushrooms, onions, peas, CREAM SAUCE) Sauté 3 slices of onion and 1 medium-size sliced mushroom together. When they are done, salt to taste and add 1 tablespoon of cooked peas and 1 tablespoon of CREAM SAUCE, although this last is optional. Mix well, and pour on the eggs.

DINARD (mushrooms, spinach, croutons, parsley, CREAM SAUCE) Sauté 1 large or 2 medium-size sliced mushrooms, add 1 tablespoon of cooked spinach and 5 or 6 croutons. Sprinkle with parsley. Add 1 tablespoon of CREAM SAUCE (optional). Mix well and proceed.

FORESTIERE (mushrooms, lardons, *fines herbes*) Sauté 1 large or 2 medium-size sliced mushrooms. When they are done, add 6 to 8 lardons. Sprinkle with *fines herbes*. Mix well and proceed.

You should be able to make easily the following variations, using the procedures and quantities listed above.

FEYDEAU (mushrooms, lardons, croutons, garlic)

JULES VERNE (mushrooms, peas, lettuce, croutons, CREAM SAUCE) 2 leaves of Boston lettuce needed here. Just cut them into the pan.

MONTE CRISTO (mushrooms, artichoke hearts, peas, rice, parsley)

NEUILLY (mushrooms, eggplant, tomatoes, basil, *fines herbes*)

NOGENT (mushrooms, green pepper, summer squash, garlic, TOMATO SAUCE)

FOUQUET (mushrooms, eggplant, lardons, *fines herbes*, TOMATO SAUCE)

VINCENNES (mushrooms, bacon, spinach, garlic, *fines herbes*)

BANDOL (mushrooms, artichoke hearts, carrots, *fines herbes*, cheese)

ST. PERAY (mushrooms, spinach, noodles, croutons, and CREAM SAUCE, which is optional)

DEAUVILLE (mushrooms, green pepper, lardons, *fines herbes*, TOMATO SAUCE)

LE TOUQUET (mushrooms, eggplant, garlic, cheese, *fines herbes*)

JUAN LES PINS (mushrooms in CREAM SAUCE, peas, croutons, cheese) Sauté 6 or 8 croutons and add the creamed mushrooms, which have been prepared ahead of time. Add 1 tablespoon of cooked peas, and proceed.

ST. MAXIME (mushrooms, tomatoes, green pepper, garlic, cheese)

RIVIERA (mushrooms, asparagus tips, croutons, truffles)

TOULON (mushrooms, artichoke hearts, peas, croutons, cheese)

PERPIGNAN (mushrooms, spinach, croutons, walnuts, cheese, CREAM SAUCE)

BONAPARTE (mushrooms, asparagus, *foie gras*, croutons, rice, SHERRY SAUCE)

TUILERIES (mushrooms, *foie gras*, truffles, croutons, cheese)

SEGUR (mushrooms, tomatoes, rice, truffles, walnuts, cheese)

CARILLON (mushrooms, *foie gras*, spinach, rice, walnuts, SHERRY SAUCE)

EDEN ROC (mushrooms, croutons, truffles, rice, almonds, MADEIRA SAUCE)

VAUGIRARD (mushrooms, croutons, walnuts, cheese, COURVOISIER SAUCE)

CHARENTAISE (mushrooms, *foie gras*, truffles, croutons, cheese, COURVOISIER SAUCE)

Sausage Omelettes

(OMELETTES AUX SAUCISSES)

When you have only two or three ingredients, use more sausage than when there are four or five ingredients.

BERCY (sausages, *fines herbes*, TOMATO SAUCE) Cut 1 or 2 sausages in pieces and toss them into the pan. If they make too much fat, pour it out and replace with butter. Shake the pan well so that the sausages are evenly cooked. Salt and pepper to taste. Add 1 tablespoon of *fines herbes* or parsley. When the omelette has been folded, pour the warmed TOMATO SAUCE over it.

PARISIENNE (sausages, tomatoes, mushrooms, *fines herbes*) Sauté 2 or 3 slices of tomato, and add 1 small mushroom cut in slices, along with 1 medium-size sausage cut in pieces. Salt and pepper. Mix well in the pan. Sprinkle with *fines herbes* or parsley.

VENDEENNE (sausages, potatoes, onions, parsley, TOMATO SAUCE) Sauté 3 slices of onion. When they are halfway done, add 4 or 5 slices of boiled potato. Shake the pan well, turning the potatoes. Now add 1 medium-size sausage cut in slices. Mix well together. Sprinkle with parsley, pour in the eggs, and when the omelette has been turned onto the plate, cover it with warm TOMATO SAUCE.

Here are some variations on the sausage omelette. Where I have not specified amounts, refer to the recipes above.

MAZARIN (sausages, mushrooms, onions, TOMATO SAUCE)

JULES ROMAIN (sausages, spinach, onions, rice, herbs) 3 slices of onion, 1 sausage cut in pieces, and 1 tablespoon each of cooked spinach and rice.

FRANCOIS COPPEE (sausages, eggplant, tomatoes, garlic, parsley) Sauté 2 slices of tomato with 5 or 6 pieces of eggplant, and add 1 sausage, cut up.

NORMANDIE (sausages, mushrooms, croutons, *fines herbes*, TOMATO SAUCE)

JEAN JACQUES ROUSSEAU (sausages, lardons, tomatoes, onions, *fines herbes*)

DE LIGNIERES (sausages, potatoes, bacon, garlic, *fines herbes*)

AUSTERLITZ (sausages, ham, potatoes, onions, parsley)

PORTE MAILLOT (sausages, eggplant, summer squash, garlic, TOMATO SAUCE)

CHAMP DE MARS (sausages, green pepper, rice, garlic, parsley, TOMATO SAUCE)

BAUDELAIRE (sausages, tomatoes, peppers, garlic, parsley, cheese)

PASSY (sausages, spinach, mushrooms, croutons, CREAM SAUCE)

CHATELET (sausages, eggplant, green pepper, onions, garlic, TOMATO SAUCE)

MARBEUF (sausages, ham, potatoes, spinach, garlic, parsley)

BATIGNOLES (sausages, ham, peas, croutons, parsley, cheese)

PIGALLE (sausages, tomatoes, peppers, summer squash, garlic, parsley)

TARASCONNE (sausages, bacon, beans, spinach, onions)

TOULOUSE (sausages, tomatoes, noodles, croutons, *fines herbes*)

CHAILLOT (sausages, ham, spinach, croutons, parsley, cheese)

PLACE DU TERTRE (sausages, apples, croutons, walnuts, CREAM SAUCE)

EPERNAY (sausages, asparagus tips, croutons, CREAM SAUCE, cheese)

ROCHECHOUART (sausages, mushrooms, truffles, parsley, cheese)

CAUMARTIN (sausages, lardons, mushrooms, croutons, walnuts, cheese)

AUBERVILLIERS (sausages, spinach, croutons, walnuts, CREAM SAUCE, cheese)

CONCORDE (sausages, lardons, truffles, rice, walnuts, cheese)

AUTEUIL (sausages, apples, croutons, walnuts, CREAM SAUCE) Sauté 5 or 6 slices of apple. Add 5 or 6 croutons and 1 sausage, cut up.

LONGCHAMPS (sausages, apples, rice, cheese)

YVONNE (sausages, croutons, *fines herbes*, garlic, TOMATO SAUCE)

Ham Omelettes

For each of these omelettes you will need about a handful of diced ham, 8 or 10 cubes.

GASCONNE (ham, onions)   Sauté 4 or 5 slices of onion. When they are done, add about 8 to 10 small pieces or cubes of ham. Mix well with a fork, pour on the eggs, and complete as usual.

PETITE FERMIERE (ham, potatoes, onions)   Begin as above with 4 or 5 slices of onion. Put them aside, then sauté 4 or 5 slices of boiled potato. When these are golden on both sides, add the onions and 5 to 8 cubes of ham. Turn well together until the ham is cooked a *little*. Then pour on the eggs and complete.

BONNE FEMME (ham, lardons, onions, croutons)   Cook the onions as above. When they are half done, add 6 cubes of ham, the same amount of lardons and of croutons. Mix well together in the pan. No salt, except what is in the eggs. Pour on the eggs and complete.

MONACO (ham, olives, croutons, tomatoes)   Sauté 3 slices of tomato in the hot butter. Add 6 or 7 cubes of ham, and the same number of croutons. Shake the pan. Cut 1 or 2 olives into the eggs and pour them on top. Finish as usual. No salt in this one except for a little on top of the tomatoes.

BEARNAISE (ham, tomatoes, onion)   Make it like the one above.

COTE D'AZUR (ham, peas, mushrooms, croutons, lettuce) Sauté 1 or 2 mushrooms cut in slices. Add 6 or 8 cubes of ham, and as many croutons, 1 tablespoon of cooked peas, and 1 or 2 leaves of lettuce (preferably Boston) cut into shreds. Salt to taste, and mix well with a fork. Pour on the eggs and complete.

MONTE CARLO (ham, asparagus tips, peas, CREAM SAUCE) Put all together in the pan 6 or 8 cubes of ham, 1 stalk of asparagus cut in pieces, 1 tablespoon of cooked peas, and 1 tablespoon of CREAM SAUCE. Mix well. Pour in the eggs and finish.

MIGNON (ham, artichoke hearts, croutons, parsley)   Take 1 tablespoonful of cooked, broken artichoke hearts and sauté with the ham and croutons. Sprinkle with parsley, mix well, and proceed.

Here are some variations on the ham omelette. Where amounts are not specified, refer to the recipes above.

GRAND DUC (ham, asparagus, rice, cheese)   8 cubes of ham, 1 stalk of asparagus, cut up, 1 tablespoon of cooked rice, 1 tablespoon of grated cheese.

BAYONNAISE (ham, spinach, croutons, CREAM SAUCE)   8 cubes of ham, the same number of croutons, 1 tablespoon of cooked spinach.

BIZET (ham, tomatoes, green pepper, onions, rice, parsley)

Sauté 6 or 8 cubes of green pepper, 2 slices of tomato, 3 slices of onion, and 1 tablespoon of rice.

DEBUSSY (ham, eggplant, onions, herbs, TOMATO SAUCE)

MOZART (ham, artichoke hearts, garlic, parsley, cheese)

VIROFLAY (ham, potatoes, spinach, oil, cheese)

CHOPIN (ham, mushrooms, croutons, garlic, cheese)

BIARRITZ (ham, mushrooms, noodles, olives, *fines herbes*)

JULIENAS (ham, potatoes, spinach, onions, parsley)

SULTANE (ham, onions, mushrooms, peas, croutons)

MONTPENSIER (ham, asparagus tips, mushrooms, parsley)

MONTSERRAT (ham, tomatoes, summer squash, rice, garlic, parsley)

MURAT (ham, spinach, mushrooms, croutons, garlic, parsley)

CLICHY (ham, asparagus, noodles, CREAM SAUCE, cheese)

PORTE ST. MARTIN (ham, eggplant, green pepper, garlic, herbs, TOMATO SAUCE)

FIGEAC (ham, tomatoes, spinach, bacon, rice, parsley)

FLAMANDE (ham, croutons, *foie gras*, cheese, MADEIRA SAUCE)

PLACE BELLECOUR (ham, croutons, *foie gras*, cheese, MADEIRA SAUCE)

LOUIS JOUVET (ham, mushrooms, spinach, croutons, *foie gras*, sherry) Sprinkle the sherry on top of the ingredients before you pour in the eggs.

MONTPARNASSE (ham, tomatoes, mushrooms, *foie gras*, cheese, SHERRY SAUCE)

ST. CLOUD (ham, mushrooms, croutons, truffles, cheese, SHERRY SAUCE)

MAYOL (ham, artichoke hearts, bacon, croutons, truffles, sherry)   Use the sherry as in the LOUIS JOUVET.

FERNANDEL (ham, *foie gras*, croutons, walnuts, cheese, MADEIRA SAUCE)

JEAN COCTEAU (ham, *foie gras*, mushrooms, truffles, walnuts, cognac)   As with the sherry, sprinkle the cognac in the pan on the ingredients and then add the eggs.

Grilled or Roast Chicken Omelettes

(OMELETTES AU POULET GRILLE)

For each one of these omelettes you will need approximately 10 to 12 small pieces of diced chicken, unless otherwise noted. These omelettes are excellent for using up chicken leftovers, and if you like them for their own sake, it is easy to put aside a piece for later omelettes whenever you cook a chicken.

Among the meat omelettes, these are the easiest to do. They are a great help to the working woman, who can buy a chicken already cooked at the store on her way home and prepare a fine meal in a very short time, and with very little trouble.

DESAUGIERS (chicken, artichoke hearts, olives, garlic)
This one is very easy. Just open 1 or 2 artichoke hearts and distribute the leaves in the hot butter. They do not have to cook: simply turn them with a fork. Now add just a little garlic and then the chicken—for this omelette, anywhere from 10 to 18 diced pieces. Mix well, cut an olive into it, and pour on the eggs.

MONTAGNE (chicken, asparagus, rice, garlic, parsley)
Make it like the one above, using asparagus instead of artichokes. Cut 1 or 2 stalks of cooked asparagus in small pieces. Drop them in the hot butter and turn them over two or three times. Add 1 tablespoon of cooked rice, a

little garlic, and then the chicken—the usual 10 to 12 pieces
this time. Mix all well with a fork and pour on the eggs.

PIERRE DUPONT (chicken, tomatoes, mushrooms, *fines
herbes*) Cut 1 medium-size mushroom in slices and sauté
in butter. Add 2 slices of tomato. Do not cut them too thin
or they will get soupy. Now add the chicken and 1 tablespoon of *fines herbes*. Mix all well together in the pan and
pour on the eggs.

ST. SAENS (chicken, mushrooms, croutons, tarragon, *fines
herbes*) Cut 1 medium-size mushroom in slices and sauté
in butter. Add 5 to 6 croutons and then the chicken. Mix
well. Salt to taste. Add now a soupçon of tarragon and 1 teaspoon of *fines herbes* or parsley. Proceed as usual.

RICHELIEU (chicken, bacon, potatoes, garlic, *fines herbes*)
Sauté about 4 to 5 slices of potato together with 4 or 5
cubes of bacon, until golden. Turn the potatoes. Now add
1 or 2 tablespoons of diced chicken and just a little garlic.
Sprinkle with *fines herbes* or parsley. Turn well with a
fork and pour on the eggs.

FLAUBERT (chicken, lardons, croutons, olives, parsley)
Proceed as in the recipe above.

EMILE ZOLA (chicken, lardons, spinach, croutons, rice,
fines herbes) Sauté the lardons and the croutons first,
5 or 6 pieces each. When they are done, add 1 tablespoon
of cooked chopped spinach and 1 tablespoon of cooked
rice. Mix well with a fork, and shake the pan. Add 1 or
2 tablespoons of diced chicken. Sprinkle with *fines herbes*
or parsley. Pour on the eggs and complete.

PRINCE DE SAGAN (chicken, ham, tomatoes, croutons,
fines herbes) Sauté 2 slices of tomato with 4 or 5 croutons

and 3 or 4 cubes of ham. Mix well together. Now add 1 or 2 tablespoons of diced chicken and mix well again. Sprinkle with the *fines herbes* or parsley, and complete.

HENRI IV (chicken, eggplant, tomatoes, garlic, *fines herbes*) Sauté about 2 slices of tomato with 4 or 5 pieces of eggplant. Cook a little—or perhaps one should say simmer. Turn them over. Salt a little. Now add the chicken and a little garlic. Sprinkle with *fines herbes* or parsley. Shake the pan and mix ingredients with a fork. Pour on the eggs and complete.

MALMAISON (chicken, spinach, mushrooms, croutons, *fines herbes*) Made like the EMILE ZOLA, using 1 medium-size mushroom cut into slices, 1 tablespoon of cooked spinach, and 4 or 5 croutons.

MONA LISA (chicken, asparagus tips, croutons, cheese) Made like the MONTAGNE.

BASTILLE (chicken, lardons, spinach, croutons, cheese) Made like the EMILE ZOLA.

LE DOYEN (chicken, tomatoes, green pepper, noodles, garlic, *fines herbes*) Take about 1 tablespoon of green pepper, cut into small cubes. Start it first, slowly, in the pan. When it is tender, add 2 slices of tomato and cook together one more minute, then add about 1 tablespoon of cooked noodles and a little garlic. Turn well together. Now add the chicken. Mix well again. Sprinkle with *fines herbes* or parsley. Pour on the eggs and complete.

ELDORADO (chicken, ham, spinach, tomatoes, croutons, cheese) Sauté 2 slices of tomato together with 4 or 5 cubes of ham. When the tomatoes are done on one side, turn them over. Add 1 tablespoon of cooked spinach and

4 or 5 croutons. Mix well together with a fork. Shake the pan. Now add 1 tablespoon of diced chicken. Mix again. Salt to taste and pour on the eggs with 1 tablespoon of grated cheese in them.

BALZAC (chicken, bacon, croutons, oyster plant, cheese) Sauté 5 or 6 pieces of oyster plant cut in small pieces, together with 5 or 6 pieces of bacon and about the same number of croutons. When they are golden, add the chicken. Do not add salt, except to the eggs. Mix well and pour on the eggs.

RENAISSANCE (chicken, artichoke hearts, mushrooms) Sauté 1 medium-size mushroom, sliced, with 1 or 2 artichoke hearts, broken. Mix these well in the hot butter. Now add approximately 1 or 2 tablespoons of diced chicken. Mix well again. Pour on the eggs and proceed.

MAINTENON (chicken, mushrooms, olives) Proceed as above, but use 2 mushrooms and a little more chicken, 10 to 12 pieces, since you have only two ingredients. I do not think of the olive as an ingredient; it is only a supplement. When chicken and mushrooms are well mixed, cut on top of them, or into the egg, 1 large or 2 small olives. Complete.

ROSTAND (chicken, asparagus, croutons, MADEIRA SAUCE) Cut 2 stalks of cooked asparagus into small pieces in hot butter. Add 5 or 6 croutons. Shake the pan well so that the asparagus is coated with the butter. Now add 8 to 10 pieces of chicken and turn with a fork. When the omelette has been folded, cover with 3 tablespoons of sauce.

LA FONTAINE (chicken, bacon, mushrooms, rice, MADEIRA SAUCE) Proceed as in the MAINTENON, only add 5 or 6 cubes of fried bacon first, then 1 medium-size sliced mushroom, and 1 tablespoon of cooked rice. Mix well. Add 8 to 10 pieces of chicken and mix again. When the omelette has been folded, cover with the sauce.

BRILLAT SAVARIN (chicken, mushrooms, peas, noodles, MADEIRA SAUCE) Sauté 1 sliced medium-size mushroom in hot butter, and add 1 tablespoon of cooked peas and 1 tablespoon of cooked noodles. Mix all this well in the pan. Add the chicken and mix again. When the omelette is on the plate, cover with 3 tablespoons of MADEIRA SAUCE.

LOUIS XIV (chicken, tomatoes, eggplant, rice, parsley, SHERRY SAUCE) Sauté 4 pieces of eggplant and 2 slices of tomato together. Salt to taste. Turn on both sides. When they are done, add 1 tablespoon of cooked rice and the chicken. Mix well. Sprinkle with a little parsley. Pour on the eggs and complete. Serve with 3 tablespoons of SHERRY SAUCE on top.

BAGATELLE (chicken and chicken livers, artichoke hearts, rice, croutons, SHERRY SAUCE) Sauté your chicken livers in separate pan. Half a liver is enough, unless it is a small one, then use the whole. In the omelette pan sauté 1 artichoke heart, cut in pieces, and 5 or 6 croutons. Add the livers, 1 tablespoon of diced chicken, and 1 tablespoon of cooked rice. Mix well with a fork. Salt to taste. Pour on the eggs and complete. Cover folded omelette with SHERRY SAUCE.

LUXEMBOURG (chicken, oyster plant, mushrooms, noodles, SHERRY SAUCE) Sauté 1 medium-size sliced mushroom with 10 pieces of diced oyster plant. Mix well. Add approximately 1 or 2 tablespoons of cooked noodles. Add the chicken, about 2 tablespoons. Salt to taste. Serve with SHERRY SAUCE.

SARAH BERNHARDT (chicken, bacon, artichoke hearts, rice, SAUCE PORTO) Sauté about 6 or 8 cubes of bacon. When they are done, add 1 or 2 medium-size artichoke hearts, cut in pieces. Add 1 tablespoon of cooked rice. Mix well. Do not salt. Add the chicken and mix all together. Pour on the eggs and complete. Serve with MADEIRA SAUCE.

MERE FILLOUX (chicken, mushrooms, truffles, rice, CREAM SAUCE) This one is named in honor of one of the most famous restaurants in Lyon, which once served the great of the world but now does not exist. Mère Filloux, the owner, was famous for her chicken Mère Filloux, which was no more than a boiled chicken made extraordinary because of a special broth and because the chicken was cooked with slices of truffles under the skin. You can see why I named this omelette after her. Sauté 2 or 3 sliced mushrooms. Add 1 tablespoon of cooked rice and 2 or 3 tablespoons of diced chicken. Mix well together. Just before putting in the eggs, add 2 or 3 slices of truffles. Serve with a CREAM SAUCE.

MERE BRAZIER (chicken, oyster plant, artichoke hearts, *foie gras*, SAUCE SUPREME) This is named for another famous restaurant in Lyon, now operated by Mère Brazier's son. Sauté 6 or 8 cubes of oyster plant in butter until golden. Add 1 or 2 artichoke hearts. Salt to taste. Add the chicken and 1 tablespoon of *foie gras*. Mix well. Serve with 4 or 5 tablespoons of SAUCE SUPREME.

TOUR EIFFEL (chicken, bacon, mushrooms, croutons, truffles, cheese) Sauté 1 large or 2 medium-size mushrooms, sliced, with 5 or 6 cubes of bacon and 5 or 6 croutons. When they are done, add 2 tablespoons of diced chicken. Mix well. Now add 2 slices of truffles, and pour on the egg mixed with grated cheese.

TOUR D'ARGENT (chicken, mushrooms, artichoke hearts, *foie gras*, Royal Combier cognac) Sauté 2 mushrooms, sliced, with 2 artichoke hearts cut in pieces. Mix well. Salt to taste. Add 1 or 2 tablespoons of diced chicken and 1 tablespoon of *foie gras*. Mix well with a fork. Now sprinkle a little cognac on top. Pour on the eggs and complete.

TABARIN (chicken and chicken livers, *foie gras*, croutons, walnuts, cheese) Sauté the liver in a separate pan. When it is done, transfer it to the omelette pan and add 2 tablespoons of diced chicken, about 6 or 8 croutons, and 1 tablespoon of *foie gras*. Mix all this well. Cut into it 1 walnut. Pour in the eggs mixed with grated cheese.

BOIS DE BOULOGNE (chicken, lardons, artichoke hearts, croutons, cheese, MADEIRA SAUCE) Sauté 5 or 6 cubes of fried bacon, 6 or 8 croutons, and 1 or 2 artichoke hearts. Now add the chicken. Mix well. Pour in the eggs mixed with grated cheese. Serve with MADEIRA SAUCE.

LA COUPOLE (chicken, sweetbreads, asparagus, mushrooms, cheese, CREAM SAUCE) Sauté 1 or 2 sliced mushrooms with 3 slices of previously parboiled sweetbread. Add 2 tablespoons of chicken and a stalk of asparagus. Salt to taste. Mix well. Pour in the eggs mixed with cheese, and serve with CREAM SAUCE.

PLAZA ATHENEE (chicken, ham, *foie gras*, tomatoes, mushrooms, MADEIRA SAUCE) Sauté 1 or 2 sliced mushrooms, 2 slices of tomato, and 4 or 5 cubes of ham. When they are done, salt very little and add the chicken. Mix well. Serve with sauce.

ODEON (chicken, apples, chestnuts, croutons, sherry) Sauté half an apple, peeled and cut in slices, in butter until golden. Use chestnuts or, if you like sweet things,

a *marron glacé*. (The latter come in cans.) You need
only one. Break it in pieces and mix with the apples. Add
8 to 10 croutons, then put in the chicken. Mix well with
a fork. Sprinkle with sherry, pour on the eggs, and complete.

Here are some variations on the chicken omelette. Let me
remind you that the ingredients remain about the same as
to quantity and proportion, unless I have noted otherwise.
With chicken or any other meat, remember that if you have
only two vegetables among the ingredients, you will need
more meat, but if you have as many as four, you will need
less. A little experimentation will provide the proper balance
that suits your own taste.

LA ROSERAIE (chicken, *foie gras*, artichoke hearts, croutons, cheese, sherry)

OREE DU BOIS (chicken, *foie gras*, mushrooms, oyster
plant, truffles, CREAM SAUCE, Courvoisier)

ROYAL HAUSSMANN (chicken, lardons, spinach, mushrooms, croutons, cheese)

CAPUCINE (chicken, sweetbreads, tomatoes, spinach, croutons, MADEIRA SAUCE)

DIRECTOIRE (chicken, lardons, oyster plant, mushrooms,
rice, CREAM SAUCE)

EDOUARD HERRIOT (chicken, *foie gras*, truffles, SAUCE
SUPREME)

CHAMPS ELYSEES (chicken, *foie gras*, chestnuts, almonds,
GRAND ARMAGNAC SAUCE)

LIDO (chicken, mushrooms, truffles, almonds, croutons,
COURVOISIER SAUCE)

PARC MONCEAU (chicken, *foie gras*, truffles, walnuts, ROYALE SAUCE)

ARMENONVILLE (chicken, apples, marrons, almonds, *fine champagne*)

ORNANO (chicken, lardons, eggplant, *fines herbes*, garlic, cheese)

BATACLAN (chicken, mushrooms, spinach, noodles, cheese) 1 medium-size mushroom, 1 tablespoon of cooked spinach, 1 tablespoon of cooked noodles, 2 tablespoons of chicken, 1 tablespoon of grated cheese in the eggs.

ROND POINT (chicken, ham, asparagus tips, peas, croutons) 4 cubes of ham, 1 stalk of asparagus, 1 tablespoon of cooked peas, 5 or 6 croutons, 2 tablespoons of chicken.

BARBES (chicken, eggplant, green pepper, garlic, *fines herbes*) 5 or 6 pieces of eggplant, 5 or 6 small pieces of pepper.

MEDRANO (chicken, artichoke hearts, bacon, mushrooms, rice) 1 artichoke heart, 4 or 5 cubes of bacon, 1 medium-size mushroom, 1 tablespoon of cooked rice.

FIDELIO (chicken, potatoes, lardons, spinach, garlic, *fines herbes*) 3 or 4 slices of potato, 5 or 6 lardons, 1 tablespoon of cooked spinach.

PAM PAM (chicken, ham, lardons, croutons, olives, cheese) 5 cubes of ham, 5 lardons, 5 or 6 croutons, 1 olive, 1 tablespoon grated cheese.

PERGOLA (chicken, tomatoes, green pepper, onions, rice, *fines herbes*) 6 or 8 cubes of green pepper, 3 slices of onion, 2 slices of tomato.

LA ROTONDE (chicken, bacon, *foie gras*, artichoke hearts, peas) 2 artichoke hearts, cut up, 1 tablespoon of cooked peas, 1 tablespoon of *foie gras*, 4 or 5 lardons.

CLOS DES LILAS (chicken, *foie gras*, mushrooms, croutons, truffles, cheese)

LA CASCADE (chicken, tomatoes, *foie gras*, croutons, olives, cheese)

LE COLOMBIER (chicken, mushrooms, artichoke hearts, truffles)

CAULINCOURT (chicken, apples, croutons, walnuts, sherry)

RAMBOUILLET (chicken, apples, almonds, croutons, cheese, sherry)

ROYAL MONCEAU (chicken, apples, *foie gras*, croutons, cheese, Courvoisier)

CAFE DE LA PAIX (chicken, *foie gras*, walnuts, mushrooms, truffles, Courvoisier)

CIRO'S (chicken, apples, *foie gras*, almonds, croutons, Grand Armagnac)

MICHODIERE (chicken, *foie gras*, artichoke hearts, truffles, croutons, Courvoisier)

CARROUSEL (chicken, apples, strawberries, walnuts, almonds, Grand Marnier)

Beef Omelettes

(OMELETTES AU BOEUF)

In these omelettes you may use any kind of leftover beef—even pieces of beef from a ragout, provided you take them out of the sauce before using. The quantity in each one will be 1 or 2 tablespoons of diced beef, depending on the number of other ingredients.

Where the recipe calls for lardons in any of these omelettes, you will need 6 to 8 cubes.

CHATEAUNEUF (beef, tomatoes, oyster plant, noodles, *fines herbes*) Sauté some diced oyster plant in butter, in a separate pan, if you prefer. Cut 2 or 3 slices of tomato into the omelette pan and cook them, turning them as you do so. Add the oyster plant and 1 tablespoon of cooked noodles. Mix well. Now add the beef, cut in small pieces. Sprinkle with the *fines herbes* and pour in the eggs.

PONTARLIER (beef, bacon, tomatoes, mushrooms, onions) Cook the bacon in a separate pan. Into the omelette pan cut 3 slices of onion, 2 slices of tomato, and half a mushroom, sliced. Cook these together, turn over, and mix well with a fork. Add the beef, mix again, and proceed.

ALEXANDRE DUMAS (beef, lardons, carrots, peas, onions, *fines herbes*) Cook the lardons in a separate pan.

Into the omelette pan cut 3 slices of onion, 1 boiled carrot cut in fine slices, and 1 tablespoon of cooked peas. Mix all this well. Now add the lardons and the beef. Sprinkle with *fines herbes* and proceed.

MOLIERE (beef, mushrooms, lardons, rice, *fines herbes*) Cook the lardons in a separate pan. Cut a whole mushroom in slices and sauté in butter. Add 1 tablespoon of cooked rice and the lardons, then the beef. Sprinkle with *fines herbes*. Mix well and proceed.

DAUDET (beef, tomatoes, onions, rice, olives, *fines herbes*) Cook together, a little slowly, 3 slices of onion and 2 slices of tomato. When they are done, add 1 tablespoon of cooked rice and the beef. Mix well. Cut in 1 or 2 olives. Sprinkle with *fines herbes*.

VALMY (beef, eggplant, green pepper, noodles, garlic, TO-MATO SAUCE) Start the peppers first, because they take a little longer to cook than the eggplant. You will need about 6 to 8 diced pieces of pepper. When they are soft, add 4 or 5 pieces of eggplant, and when these are cooked, add 1 tablespoon of cooked noodles, a hint of garlic, and the beef. Mix all well in the pan. When the omelette is folded, cover with 2 tablespoons of warm TOMATO SAUCE.

CLERMONT (beef, peas, onions, asparagus, lardons, SHERRY SAUCE) Make it like the ALEXANDRE DUMAS, but put in 1 stalk of cooked and cut asparagus instead of the carrot. When the omelette has been folded, cover with 3 table-spoons of SHERRY SAUCE.

DESMOULINS (beef, artichoke hearts, lardons, peas, MA-DEIRA SAUCE) Do the lardons separately. Break 2 artichoke hearts into the hot butter in the omelette pan. Shake the pan so that they cook a little and add 1 tablespoon of cooked peas. Now add the lardons and the beef. Mix all these well in the pan, turning with a fork. When the omelette has been folded, cover with 3 tablespoons of MADEIRA SAUCE.

GERARDMER (beef, mushrooms, artichoke hearts, noodles, SHERRY SAUCE) Cut 1 medium-size mushroom in slices and sauté in the pan, together with 2 artichoke hearts broken into small pieces. Add 1 tablespoon or more of cooked noodles. Add the beef. Mix well with a fork. Cover the completed omelette with SHERRY SAUCE.

CHATEAUBRIAND (beef, lardons, mushrooms, olives, SAUCE CHATEAUBRIAND) Do the lardons separately. In the omelette pan sauté 2 mushrooms cut in slices. When they are done, add the lardons and the beef, mixing well in the pan. Cut 2 olives either into the eggs or into the pan. Cover the completed omelette with the sauce.

METROPOLE (beef, *foie gras*, truffles, artichoke hearts, COURVOISIER SAUCE) Break 2 or 3 artichoke hearts into hot butter, shaking the pan so that they cook a little. Add 1 tablespoon of *foie gras* and the beef. Mix well with a fork. Just before you pour in the eggs, add 2 or 3 slices of truffles. Cover the completed omelette with the COURVOISIER SAUCE, or, if you prefer, CHICKEN SAUCE.

BEAUVAIS (beef, *foie gras*, mushrooms, lardons, walnuts, COURVOISIER SAUCE) Follow the procedure as in the CHATEAUBRIAND and METROPOLE. Add 1 or 2 walnuts, broken, just before putting in the eggs. Cover folded omelette with sauce.

CHATEAU D'IF (beef, *foie gras*, tomatoes, croutons, mushrooms, MADEIRA SAUCE) Slice 1 mushroom and sauté it with 4 or 5 croutons and 2 slices of tomato. When they are cooked, add the beef and 1 tablespoon of *foie gras*. Mix well. Serve with the sauce.

MAXIM'S (beef, *foie gras*, mushrooms, truffles, walnuts, rice, COURVOISIER SAUCE) Sauté 1 large mushroom, cut in slices. Add the beef and 1 tablespoon of *foie gras*. Mix well. Now cut in 2 or 3 slices of truffles, also break in bits of 2 walnuts and add 1 tablespoon of cooked rice. Mix well, and pour in the eggs immediately. Serve with sauce.

DANTON (beef, bacon, spinach, mushrooms, croutons, cheese) Prepare the croutons and bacon separately from the other ingredients, but not together, since the latter takes a little longer to cook. Into the omelette pan slice a mushroom and sauté it; then add 1 tablespoon of cooked spinach. Now add the lardons, croutons, and the beef. Mix well. Don't forget to put 1 tablespoon of grated cheese into the eggs.

In the above omelettes with croutons, I think it is better to do the croutons separately and add them just before finishing the omelette.

Veal Omelettes

(OMELETTES AU VEAU)

A friend of mine tells me that no one can cook veal the way I do. That may be the exaggeration of a friend, but I do think it is a shame that Americans do not seem to like veal, because when it is well prepared a veal roast is delicious. There is one thing to remember about cooking veal: in order to be good, it must be *well cooked*. For these omelettes, use leftovers from a roast or a cooked veal chop will do very well. The quantity of veal will be 1 or 2 tablespoons, diced, depending on the number of other ingredients.

LAMARTINE (veal, mushrooms, tomatoes, rice, parsley, cheese) Cut 1 mushroom into slices and sauté in butter with 2 slices of tomato. Add 1 tablespoon of cooked rice. Now add the veal. Mix well. Sprinkle a little parsley on top. Put 1 tablespoon of grated cheese into the eggs and make the omelette.

DE BALZAC (veal, sausages, tomatoes, green pepper, garlic, *fines herbes*) Dice 6 or 8 pieces of pepper and start cooking them first in the pan; then add 2 slices of tomato. Now add 1 sausage, cut in pieces, the veal, a little garlic, and the *fines herbes*. Salt and pepper to taste. Mix all this well with a fork, and complete.

SUFFREN (veal, eggplant, tomatoes, rice, olives, garlic, pars-

ley)   Cook together 2 slices of tomato and 5 or 6 pieces of
eggplant. When they are done, add 1 tablespoon of cooked
rice, then the veal, a little garlic, and sprinkle with parsley.
Salt and pepper to taste. Mix well and finish.

RACINE (veal, lardons, spinach, mushrooms, croutons)
Do the lardons separately, then the croutons, 6 or 8 pieces
of each. Slice and sauté 1 mushroom in the omelette pan.
Add 1 tablespoon of cooked spinach. Add the lardons and
croutons. Salt and pepper to taste. Mix well, add the veal,
and mix again. Pour on the eggs and complete.

CORNEILLE (veal, carrots, eggplant, summer squash, *fines
herbes*, TOMATO SAUCE)   Sauté in hot butter 4 or 5 pieces
of eggplant, 4 or 5 slices of squash, and 1 cooked carrot,
sliced fine. When they are cooked and soft, add the veal.
Mix well together. Sprinkle with some parsley. Serve with
the TOMATO SAUCE.

SULLY (veal, tomatoes, spinach, onions, lardons, CREAM
SAUCE)   Do the lardons separately. In the omelette pan
sauté 3 slices of onion and 2 slices of tomato. When they
are done, add 1 tablespoon of cooked spinach. Add the
lardons and the veal. Mix well. Cover the completed omelette with CREAM SAUCE.

Here are some variations on the veal omelette. The quantities
are the same as in the omelettes above.

JACOBIN (veal, *foie gras*, mushrooms, truffles, rice, MA-
DEIRA SAUCE)

DUHAMEL (veal, *foie gras*, artichoke hearts, croutons, truffles, SHERRY SAUCE)

JACQUEMARD (veal, bacon, oyster plant, croutons, mushrooms, CREAM SAUCE)

HERMITAGE (veal, oyster plant, bacon, croutons, cheese, SHERRY SAUCE)

MENTON (veal, *foie gras,* croutons, mushrooms, walnuts, COURVOISIER SAUCE)

MORLAIX (veal, *foie gras,* mushrooms, truffles, rice, MADEIRA SAUCE)

PONTOISE (veal, ham, tomatoes, spinach, onions, MADEIRA SAUCE)

Calf's-Brain Omelettes

(OMELETTES A LA CERVELLE)

Eating calf's brains is an acquired taste, but if those who have never had them will only conquer their prejudices and try, they will find them delicious.

You will need only one calf's brain for an omelette. Soak it in cold water for an hour, then drain and rinse, cut out the membranes, and put it in boiling water. Add a little lemon juice and salt. Simmer it gently for about fifteen minutes, then drain it and cover with very cold water, letting it stand until cool. Then drain it again and you are ready to prepare any of the omelettes which follow.

The proportion of calf's brain in these omelettes is the same as in all the other meat omelettes, varying according to the number of other ingredients.

CHIMAY (calf's brain, croutons, *fines herbes*, cheese) Cut in slices a calf's brain previously prepared and cooked, and sauté the slices in butter. Add 5 or 6 croutons. When both are nicely golden, add some *fines herbes* and a little salt. Be sure to add 1 tablespoon of grated cheese to the eggs before you pour them in.

ROUGET DE LISLE (calf's brain, mushrooms, croutons, *fines herbes*) Sauté 1 mushroom in slices, add the calf's brain, also 5 or 6 croutons. Turn these together. Salt a little. Sprinkle with *fines herbes*, pour in the eggs, and proceed.

SCARAMOUCHE (calf's brain, artichoke hearts, mushrooms, SHERRY SAUCE) Sauté 1 sliced mushroom with 1 artichoke heart, cut in pieces. Add the calf's brain. Sauté together a few minutes. Salt to taste. Mix well. Serve with SHERRY SAUCE.

PROVENCE (calf's brain, tomatoes, mushrooms, *fines herbes*, cheese) Sauté 1 sliced mushroom and a few slices of tomato. Cook together. Add the calf's brain, sautéed on both sides. Add some *fines herbes*. Mix well. Pour in the eggs mixed with grated cheese, and finish.

ROUVILLE (calf's brain, asparagus tips, croutons, cheese, CREAM SAUCE) Sauté the calf's brain well until golden. Add 1 stalk of asparagus cut in pieces, and 5 or 6 croutons. Salt to taste. Mix well. Pour in the eggs mixed with grated cheese, and finish. Cover with the CREAM SAUCE.

These are a few variations on the calf's-brain omelette. For quantities, see the omelettes above.

THOMASSIN (calf's brain, mushrooms, spinach, croutons, SHERRY SAUCE)

TOLOZAN (calf's brain, lardons, peas, mushrooms, SHERRY SAUCE)

FERRANDIERE (calf's brain, tomato, artichoke, peas, MADEIRA SAUCE)

CONDORCET (calf's brain, mushrooms, artichoke hearts, peas, SHERRY SAUCE)

JEAN MACE (calf's brain, artichoke hearts, peas, SHERRY SAUCE)

JEAN BART (calf's brain, mushrooms, lardons, spinach, croutons, CREAM SAUCE)

Sweetbread Omelettes

(OMELETTES AU RIZ DE VEAU)

Like calf's brains, sweetbreads are not relished by everyone, but again it is simply a matter of prejudice. It is not for nothing that sweetbreads are so often referred to by gourmets as "the dish of kings." The uninitiated should never forgive themselves if they leave this world without tasting sweetbreads.

To prepare sweetbreads, soak them in very cold water for an hour, then blanch for about fifteen minutes in simmering salt water, white wine, or wine and water; some people prefer to use water to which a little vinegar or lemon juice has been added—just enough to make it acid. Plunge the cooked sweetbreads into cold water again. This will keep them white and firm. When the sweetbreads have cooled, remove the membranes and the little tube which connects the two parts.

You will need 5 or 6 slices of cooked sweetbreads for each of these omelettes.

MERVEILLEUSE (sweetbreads, lardons, spinach, rice, SHERRY SAUCE) Do the lardons, 4 or 5 of them, in a separate pan. In the omelette pan, sauté 5 or 6 slices of sweetbreads, previously cooked. When the slices are golden on both sides, add 1 tablespoon of cooked spinach, 1 tablespoon of cooked rice, then the lardons. Mix well with a fork. Salt very little. Pour the eggs on top and finish. When the omelette has been folded, cover with the sauce.

TRIOMPHE (sweetbreads, mushrooms, tomatoes, rice, SHERRY SAUCE) Sauté 1 medium-size mushroom cut in slices and 2 slices of tomato. Then add 4 to 6 slices of cooked sweetbreads, and 1 tablespoon of cooked rice. Salt to taste. Mix well with a fork. When the omelette has been folded, cover with 3 to 4 tablespoons of the sauce.

ROUSSILLON (sweetbreads, asparagus tips, peas, mushrooms, SHERRY SAUCE) Sauté 1 medium-size mushroom, sliced. Add to it 1 stalk of cooked asparagus, cut in small pieces, 1 tablespoon of cooked peas, and 4 to 6 slices of cooked sweetbreads. Mix all this well in the pan, turning the sweetbreads. Salt to taste. When the omelette is folded, cover with the sauce.

REAUMUR (sweetbreads, lardons, artichoke hearts, croutons) Do the lardons in a separate pan. In the omelette pan, sauté the sweetbreads, 4 or 5 slices of them. Turn on both sides. Salt to taste. Add 2 artichoke hearts, broken in pieces, and 4 or 5 croutons. Add the lardons. Mix all this well with a fork. Pour the eggs on top and complete.

CHAMPERET (sweetbreads, asparagus tips, mushrooms, cheese, CREAM SAUCE) Sauté 1 sliced mushroom, then add 4 to 6 slices of the sweetbreads. Salt to taste. Add 1 stalk of cooked asparagus, cut in small pieces. Mix all this with a fork. Pour in the eggs mixed with grated cheese, and complete. Cover folded omelette with the sauce.

VALERY (sweetbreads, tomatoes, spinach, croutons, cheese, SHERRY SAUCE) Sauté 2 slices of tomato in the pan, along with 4 or 5 slices of sweetbreads, 1 tablespoon of cooked spinach, and 4 or 5 croutons. Mix well with a fork, add the eggs and grated cheese. Cover with sauce.

RAMPONEAU (sweetbreads, tomatoes, mushrooms, croutons, rice, cheese) Made like the TRIOMPHE.

RAIMU (sweetbreads, *foie gras*, mushrooms, MADEIRA SAUCE) Sauté 1 sliced mushroom with 5 or 6 slices of sweetbreads. When they are done on both sides, add 1 tablespoon of *foie gras*. Salt to taste. Mix well. Pour the eggs on top and proceed. When the omelette is folded, cover with sauce.

Here are a few variations on the sweetbread omelettes. For quantities, see the recipes above.

D'AUBIGNY (sweetbreads, asparagus tips, lardons, croutons, cheese)

JACQUARD (sweetbreads, mushrooms, croutons, truffles, MADEIRA SAUCE)

TAILLEVENT (sweetbreads, bacon, oyster plant, cheese, SHERRY SAUCE)

GIRAUDOUX (sweetbreads, *foie gras*, artichoke hearts, truffles, SAUCE SUPREME)

SAUMUR (sweetbreads, *foie gras*, oyster plant, croutons, truffles, COURVOISIER SAUCE)

LAMOTHE (sweetbreads, ham, mushrooms, oyster plant, croutons, cheese, COURVOISIER SAUCE)

Calf's-Liver Omelettes

(OMELETTES AU FOIE DE VEAU)

For these omelettes you have to prepare the calf's liver before-hand. Since this liver is easily and quickly cooked, you will have no trouble preparing it at the last minute. For each of these omelettes, 6 to 8 small cubes of liver will be enough.

ROBINSON (calf's liver, onions, spinach, croutons, cheese) Sauté 3 slices of onion in the omelette pan. When it is done, add 1 tablespoon of cooked spinach, 4 or 5 croutons, and 6 to 8 pieces of diced cooked calf's liver. If the liver is hot, make the omelette right away; if it is cold, just turn once or twice. Mix all with a fork. Salt to taste. Pour in the eggs mixed with grated cheese and complete.

CHAROLLAISE (calf's liver, lardons, tomatoes, eggplant, garlic, *fines herbes*) Do the lardons in a separate pan. In the omelette pan sauté 2 slices of tomato and 4 to 6 pieces of an eggplant. Cook together. When they are done, add the calf's liver, the lardons, a little garlic, and sprinkle on *fines herbes*.

MACONNAISE (calf's liver, mushrooms, croutons, onions, SHERRY SAUCE) Sauté 3 slices of onion till golden. Add 1 sliced mushroom and 4 or 5 croutons. Salt to taste. Now add the calf's liver. Mix well with a fork. When the omelette has been folded, cover with the sauce.

CHINON (calf's liver, lardons, onions, rice, *fines herbes*, TO-MATO SAUCE) Do the lardons separately. In the omelette pan, sauté 3 slices of onion. When they are golden, add 1 tablespoon of cooked rice. Add the calf's liver and the lardons. Sprinkle with *fines herbes*. Mix all this well with a fork. When the omelette is folded, cover with TOMATO SAUCE.

Here are a half-dozen variations on the calf's-liver omelette. The quantities will be the same as in the omelettes above.

PASCAL (calf's liver, lardons, onions, croutons, peas, SHERRY SAUCE)

ROUBAIX (calf's liver, eggplant, tomatoes, green pepper, garlic, *fines herbes*)

RONSARD (calf's liver, artichoke hearts, lardons, MADEIRA SAUCE)

JUSSIEU (calf's liver, mushrooms, onions, spinach, croutons, SHERRY SAUCE)

ROYANS (calf's liver, bacon, oyster plant, rice, croutons, SHERRY SAUCE)

GOBELINS (calf's liver, oyster plant, croutons, cheese, *fines herbes*, CREAM SAUCE)

Omelettes of Various Kinds

Lobster Omelettes (OMELETTES AU HOMARD)

If you don't want to prepare a fresh lobster, you may buy it in cans or use the frozen variety.

THERMIDOR (lobster, mushrooms, olives, *fines herbes*, CREAM SAUCE) Sauté 1 medium-size sliced mushroom, then add the lobster, about 8 to 10 pieces the size of a nickel. Mix together. Sprinkle with *fines herbes* or parsley. Cut 2 olives into the eggs or into the pan before you pour. When the omelette has been folded, cover with CREAM SAUCE.

VERNAY (lobster, tomatoes, lardons, olives, cheese, SHERRY SAUCE) Prepare like other omelettes involving the same ingredients.

A few variations on the lobster omelette:

D'ARSONVAL (lobster, mushrooms, tomatoes, rice, *fines herbes*, tarragon)

TURENNE (lobster, mushrooms, artichoke hearts, truffles, SHERRY SAUCE)

NEUVILLE (lobster, mushrooms, croutons, rice, cream, Courvoisier) Sprinkle 2 or 3 drops of the Courvoisier in the omelette.

BEAUCAIRE (lobster, mushrooms, tomatoes, truffles, cheese, Courvoisier)

MIRABEAU (lobster, mushrooms, croutons, truffles, CREAM SAUCE)

DENISE (lobster, tomatoes, olives, croutons, truffles, COURVOISIER SAUCE)

FEUILLAT (lobster, bacon, mushrooms, croutons, cheese, CREAM SAUCE)

Omelettes with Caviar

CEZANNE (caviar, onions, lardons, olives, parsley) For these *omelettes au caviar*, chop the onion, about 1 tablespoon, but not too fine; don't slice it, as in the other omelettes. Do the lardons in a separate pan. Put the chopped onion in the omelette pan, but don't cook it too much; I prefer it almost raw. If the lardons are ready, drop them in. Do not add salt, only pepper. Pour the eggs on top and cook the omelette halfway. Lower the flame at this point. Now add 1 tablespoon of caviar, distributing it evenly. Cut in 1 olive. Finish the omelette, which should be done by the time you put in the caviar. Sprinkle with parsley.

MICHELET (mushrooms, onions, croutons, caviar) Slice a mushroom and sauté it with the onions, done as above, adding 5 or 6 croutons. Then follow the same procedure as above.

SERIGNAN (caviar, croutons, olives, truffles, and walnuts) This one I created especially for *Life* magazine.

VAUBAN (caviar, onions, croutons, truffles, bacon)

JOURDAN (caviar, ham, bacon, onions, mushrooms, cheese)

Tuna-Fish Omelettes

JUSSERAND (tuna fish, potatoes, onions, *fines herbes*, CREAM SAUCE) Sauté about 4 or 5 slices of boiled potato, together with 1 tablespoon of chopped onions (done like the ones in the CEZANNE). Add 1 small tablespoon of tuna fish (canned), broken in pieces. Mix well. Sprinkle with *fines herbes*. When the omelette has been folded, cover with CREAM SAUCE.

ST. REMY (tuna fish, potatoes, onions, olives, parsley, cheese) Make it as above, adding the olive and the grated cheese in the eggs.

TIVOLI (tuna fish, tomatoes, onions, parsley, CREAM SAUCE)

Salmon Omelettes

EPINAY (salmon, potatoes, spinach, cheese) Sauté 4 or 5 slices of boiled potato until golden, then add 1 tablespoon of chopped cooked spinach and 1 tablespoon of cooked salmon. Add 1 tablespoon of grated cheese to the eggs.

RAYNOUARD (salmon, mushrooms, rice, cheese, CREAM SAUCE)

ST. DENIS (salmon, mushrooms, croutons, rice, truffles, SHERRY SAUCE)

Omelettes au Foie Gras

The amount of *foie gras* in these omelettes depends on how rich you like them, but about 1 tablespoon is usual.

LUCULLUS (*foie gras*, mushrooms, croutons, cheese) Sauté 1 medium to large sliced mushroom. When nicely done, add 5 or 6 croutons and 1 tablespoon of *foie gras*. Turn everything with a fork, and pour on the eggs with the grated cheese immediately.

ORLY (*foie gras*, artichoke hearts, mushrooms, croutons, walnuts, COURVOISIER SAUCE) Sauté 1 sliced mushroom together with 2 artichoke hearts broken in pieces. When they are done, add 5 or 6 croutons. Mix well with a fork. Now add the *foie gras*, about 1 tablespoon. Mix again and pour on the eggs. Add 1 or 2 walnuts cut in pieces, and finish the omelette. When it has been folded, cover with COURVOISIER SAUCE.

COQ HARDI (*foie gras*, mushrooms, croutons, truffles, cheese, COURVOISIER SAUCE) Same as above.

BOBINO (*foie gras*, apples, croutons, walnuts, cheese, GRAND ARMAGNAC SAUCE) Sauté 6 or 8 slices of apple and 6 to 8 croutons. Turn the apples on the other side. Add the *foie gras*, as above, and 2 broken walnuts. Now pour on the eggs and grated cheese. When the omelette is folded, cover with the sauce.

PALAIS ROYAL (*foie gras*, croutons, truffles, walnuts, almonds, cheese, GRAND MARNIER SAUCE)

ARC DE TRIOMPHE (*foie gras*, mushrooms, truffles, pistachio nuts, Courvoisier) Sprinkle a few drops of Courvoisier in the pan before adding the eggs.

OLYMPIA (*foie gras*, apples, chestnuts, croutons, *fine champagne*)

JOCONDE (*foie gras*, croutons, pistachio nuts, almonds, cheese, GRAND ARMAGNAC SAUCE)

PERIGORD (*foie gras*, truffles flavored with madeira and Pernod) For this one, mash 2 tablespoons of *foie gras* in a bowl with 1 teaspoon of madeira and 1 teaspoon of Pernod. Make the omelette first, then add the *foie gras* and 1 small truffle before folding.

Postscripts:

I will add four recipes which do not seem to fit anywhere else. The first is so Lyonnaise that I doubt if anyone in America will be persuaded to make it, but I add it as an example of real regional French cooking, and to honor the excellent newspaper in my home city for which it is named.

OMELETTE LE PROGRES DE LYON (quenelles, rooster combs, mushrooms, truffles, pistachios, and COURVOISIER SAUCE)

Now here are three others:

FLAMMARION (quenelles, mushrooms, truffles, cheese, CREAM SAUCE)

.

HERBOUVILLE (beef, bacon, tomatoes, carrots, peas, cheese, *fines herbes*)

AMPERE (oyster plant, croutons, bacon, peas, CREAM SAUCE)

Sauces

You may think it strange to begin the discussion of sauces by telling you how to cook a chicken in wine sauce, but in giving you this basic recipe I am, at the same time, giving you the information you will need to make many other sauces.

POULET AU VIN. You will need a chicken of about 4 pounds, cut into pieces. If you do not know how to do this, the butcher will do it for you. Wash and dry the pieces. In a large stew pan put at least ¼ pound of butter, in order to make a large quantity of sauce. Now put the chicken in and cook until all the pieces have turned a nice golden brown color. Do this on a medium flame and turn the pieces around very often so that they will brown evenly. This will take from 30 to 45 minutes.

Now reduce your fire while you take the chicken out and put it aside. Put 1 full cup of flour into the stew pan, turn up the flame to medium, and let the flour turn a golden color, but not too brown, always stirring it. If you see that there is not enough butter to absorb the flour, add a little more. Add about 1 pint of stock or water, slowly at first, turning the mixture meanwhile, then a little more rapidly. Then add 2 cups of dry white wine. Salt and pepper to taste, and put the chicken back in for about 15 minutes more, reducing the fire so that it cooks very slowly.

When the chicken is done, put half of it in a dish with a little sauce, and put away the rest of the sauce in a container for future use. I will tell you how to keep that sauce for months. When it is in the container, pour on top a good half inch of melted fat. Close the container tightly, and the sauce will keep for as long as you wish. Whenever you want to use a little for a sauce, go around the edge with a knife and take out the cover of fat. You can put that same cover back again if you warm it up and pour it as before. It is air that spoils everything.

With this sauce as a base, you will have the primary ingredient for these other sauces:

SHERRY SAUCE, by adding to the basic sauce a small glass of sherry

MADEIRA SAUCE, by using madeira instead of sherry

COURVOISIER SAUCE, by using Courvoisier cognac

GRAND ARMAGNAC SAUCE, by adding Grand Armagnac

SAUCE SUPREME, by adding to the COURVOISIER SAUCE 1 tablespoon of heavy cream and a few slices of cooked mushrooms.

One word of caution: When you take the sauce out of the jar, it may be a little thick. If so, when you warm it up, add a little more white wine.

Another caution: All the sauces should be strained before they are used to cover an omelette, or for anything else.

Here are a few other variations, using the basic sauce:

SAUCE CHASSEUR   Add some slices of mushroom, but no liquor, to the sauce. Also add a little more white wine and about 2 tablespoons of TOMATO SAUCE.

ROYALE SAUCE   To the SAUCE SUPREME, add a little Armagnac and a few pieces of truffle. Omit the cream.

BORDELAISE SAUCE I   Add a small glass of red wine, with a little thyme, a small piece of laurel leaf, and a bit of chopped shallot.

CHAMPAGNE SAUCE   As you may have suspected, add champagne to the basic sauce.

The moral of the above recipes is this: if you want to have a good sauce, you must have a good base. A chef would spend three or four hours preparing such a base, and that is why I have explained this basic white wine sauce, which is simple enough for those who are not *artistes* in the kitchen—and the more complicated sauces do require such an *artiste*, otherwise everyone would be able to cook like an accomplished *chef de cuisine*.

"But, madame," you may say, "do I always have to cook a chicken in order to obtain this sauce?" Certainly not, but I must warn you that a sauce made otherwise will not have that special taste which the POULET AU VIN recipe lends to it.

Now here is another kind of basic sauce:

BLOND SAUCE   It will not have the same taste as the sauce with chicken, but it will have a good taste of its own when something is added to it. In making this sauce, or any other, never use a light pan. A heavy pan is always necessary. Put in 2 tablespoons of butter (or any fat) and let it melt. Add 2 tablespoons of flour, turning constantly with a wooden spoon until it is golden. Gradually and slowly at first, add 1 cup of stock, if you have it. If not, water will do. If the mixture is too thin, let it simmer a little. If too thick, add more stock or water. Salt and pepper to taste.

With this basic sauce you can make the following:

CREAM SAUCE Add 2 tablespoons of heavy cream to BLOND SAUCE.

SAUCE *FINES HERBES* Chop 3 or 4 sprigs of parsley very fine. Add a little chervil and a pinch of tarragon, also a little lemon juice.

OYSTER SAUCE Add oyster water when you cook the BLOND SAUCE.

BORDELAISE SAUCE II A different Bordelaise from the one previously listed. Chop 2 shallots very fine and sauté them in a pan with butter until they are transparent. Add this to the BLOND SAUCE, with a small glass of Bordeaux wine, either white or red. Add 1 teaspoon of chopped parsley. Salt and pepper to taste.

LYONNAISE SAUCE In a pan with butter brown 1 small onion, chopped very fine. Add this to the BLOND SAUCE, also 1 tablespoon of vinegar. This sauce is very good with leftover beef.

BROWN SAUCE (*Sauce Rousse*) Made exactly the same as the BLOND SAUCE except that you let the flour become quite dark in color, well browned. Salt and pepper to taste. If you put some olives in it and some little gherkins cut in slices, you will have a sauce that is particularly good on leftover veal. If you add 1 teaspoon of mustard, you will have a SAUCE CHARCUTIERE. And by adding 1 tablespoon of tomato juice you will have TOMATO SAUCE.

SAUCE BOURGUIGNONNE   Made exactly like the BORDELAISE SAUCE II, but add red Burgundy wine and also what we call a *bouquet garni*, meaning 4 or 5 sprigs of parsley, half a bay leaf, a little thyme, and 1 clove. Salt and pepper to taste. Let this simmer and then strain the sauce.

BECHAMEL SAUCE, or WHITE SAUCE   Prepare it exactly like the BLOND SAUCE, except that the flour should not color. To prevent this, as soon as the butter and flour have been mixed, begin to add 1 cup of milk—hot is better than cold—stirring all the time with a wooden spoon, and adding the milk slowly.

SAUCE VELOUTE   This is made with the BLOND SAUCE as a base. In a pan over a low fire put the yolks of 2 eggs, stirring with a spoon until smooth. Add very slowly some of the sauce, always stirring. Do not let boil. Add 2 tablespoons of cream. Salt and pepper to taste.

SAUCE CHATEAUBRIAND   This sauce is made by cooking beef exactly as the chicken is cooked in POULET AU VIN. When the beef has browned, take it out and set it aside. Then put some flour in the pan and let it become a nice light brown. If you do not want a thick sauce, add only 3 tablespoons of flour in the butter. When the flour is browned, pour in, slowly at first, either stock or water, no more than ½ cup of it, and then a glass of Burgundy red wine. Add a little thyme and a laurel leaf, 1 clove, salt and pepper to taste. I also add some slices of onion, previously sautéed in butter.

Sweet Omelettes

(OMELETTES SUCREES)

For these sweet omelettes I have given the recipes simplest to follow. Many people are afraid to make these desserts because the recipes they have seen are so complicated, calling for two or three thin omelettes, one on top of the other, or else requiring you to break the eggs separately, as for a soufflé.

Why should there be so much trouble? Just make an omelette like any of the others, and I will guarantee your success. All of the omelettes which follow use the plain *omelette sucrée*, which I will give you first.

OMELETTE SUCREE (sweet omelette) This is the PLAIN OMELETTE described at the beginning of the recipes, with the difference that you put a tiny pinch of salt and 1 tablespoon of sugar in the eggs. Be sure the butter is nicely golden brown. It gives a good taste to the eggs. Now make the omelette, and when it has been folded, sprinkle with another tablespoon of sugar. Put it quickly under a very hot broiler to glaze it.

OMELETTE BAR-LE-DUC (currant jelly) Bar-le-duc is a brand of currant jelly, but you may use any kind you like, and any flavor. Make the omelette exactly as above, but before folding, add in the center whatever jam you are using. Sprinkle with sugar and glaze it quickly under the hot broiler.

DELICIEUSE (apples and chestnuts)   To make this one, you can use either chestnuts in syrup or *marrons glacés* (glazed chestnuts, available in most gourmet shops). Peel and core an apple and cut a few slices. For an individual omelette, 5 or 6 slices should be enough. Put them in hot butter and let them brown slightly. In the meantime, break 1 or 2 chestnuts into small pieces. The eggs you have already prepared, as for the PLAIN OMELETTE. Pour the eggs on top of the apples, and when the omelette is half done, add the chestnuts and finish. Sprinkle with sugar and glaze.

SOUVERAINE (with mixed fruits)   Make this one with a compote of fresh fruits, like apricots, plums, peaches, etc.

FEU FOLLET   This is the rum omelette. When you make the OMELETTE SUCREE, add 1 tablespoon of rum to the eggs. Make the omelette, and when it has been folded, sprinkle on 2 tablespoons of sugar and 4 or 5 tablespoons of warm rum. Be sure the rum is warm, or it will not burn. Set the rum afire and keep spooning it over the omelette until the fire dies out. This may be done at the table while you are serving, and makes quite a spectacular showpiece.

CHERUBIN (pistachio nuts, with pistachio liqueur)   Make the OMELETTE SUCREE, and before folding, add 2 tablespoons of pistachio nuts, then sprinkle with pistachio liqueur.

MARQUISE (fresh oranges and curaçao)   Peel and open an orange. Take about 8 or 10 slices and steep them in a little curaçao. Make the OMELETTE SUCREE and, before folding, add these slices in the center. When it has been folded, sprinkle with sugar and 3 tablespoons of curaçao. You can also add 1 tablespoon of orange juice to the eggs.

REVE DORE (pineapple and kirsch) Look for a French product called *ananas au kirsch* (pineapples in kirsch), but if you cannot find it, use the regular crushed pineapple in syrup, and the ordinary bottle of kirsch. Break up some pineapple and put it in the center of your omelette. When the omelette has been folded, sprinkle with sugar and 2 or 3 tablespoons of kirsch.

ARLEQUIN (filberts and CHOCOLATE SAUCE) Filberts are also called hazelnuts in this country. Cut some and garnish the center of the omelette. When it has been folded, cover with CHOCOLATE SAUCE.

CHOCOLATE SAUCE Take 2 squares of chocolate and melt them with a little water and sugar, 1 or 2 tablespoons. If the mixture is too thin, let it stay on the fire a little longer. Pour it hot on the omelette. You can make it more glossy by adding a little fresh sweet butter, but only when it is off the fire.

NORMANDE (apples and calvados) For this one, steep 1 dozen slices of apple in calvados (called applejack in America) for 15 to 20 minutes. Put these slices into the pan in hot butter and let them become golden. Sprinkle with a little sugar. Pour the eggs on top and finish the omelette. Sprinkle the top with sugar and 2 or 3 tablespoons of calvados. If you do not have calvados, use brandy.

OPERA (macaroons and jam) Crush 2 large macaroons and put them in the butter. Turn with a fork. Now pour the eggs on top and do your omelette. Before folding, add 2 tablespoons of currant jam. Sprinkle with sugar and 2 tablespoons of kirsch.

CAPRICE D'AMOUR (toasted almonds, raspberry and currant jelly) For this you can use the blanched slivered almonds which come in cans. I use them myself. When the butter is hot, put in a heaping tablespoon of these almonds and let them turn golden. Then pour the eggs and make the omelette. Before folding, put in 1 tablespoon of each of the jellies. Complete as with the others.

POMPADOUR (fresh strawberries) Clean and wash about a dozen strawberries, and let them stand on a towel to dry a little. Then put them in a bowl with 2 tablespoons of sugar and some lemon juice. Let them stand for half an hour, then add some Grand Marnier liqueur and let stand again for 10 more minutes. Make your plain OMELETTE SUCREE and before folding add the strawberries to the center. When the omelette has been folded, add more sugar and the juice you have used to marinate the strawberries. Add more Grand Marnier, too, if you wish.

SUPREME (chestnuts and CHOCOLATE SAUCE) Again, use either *marrons glacés* (glazed chestnuts, available in most gourmet shops) or those in syrup. Break about 4 or 5 of these marrons in small pieces, do your omelette, and place them in the center. When the omelette has been folded, cover with CHOCOLATE SAUCE.

MEPHISTO (candied angelica, grapes, and Pernod) Before doing the omelette, make a compote with a small bunch of white seedless grapes, using ½ cup of water and ½ cup of sugar. Stew them slowly so that they will not break open. Now prepare the eggs as in the PLAIN OMELETTE, with a small pinch of salt and 2 tablespoons of sugar. In the butter, put about 1 tablespoon or a little more of candied angelica, chopped, not necessarily fine. Turn with a fork 2 or 3 times, then pour the eggs on top.

Before folding, add some of the grapes. Sprinkle with a little sugar and 3 tablespoons of Pernod, flambé it, and serve surrounded with the remaining grapes.

FANTAISIE GLACIALE (mint leaves and green crème de menthe) Chop a few fresh mint leaves. Make the omelette, then add the mint before folding. When folded, cover with 2 tablespoons of green crème de menthe.

I might add to this discussion of sweet omelettes that you should look for the French fruits in liqueur that some stores have now. You can cut these into small pieces and put them in the center of your omelette. Then add cognac on top and flambé it. Remember that it will not burn unless it is heated first, or the plate under the omelette is very hot. There must also be plenty of sugar on top of the omelette. Be sure, too, when it is flaming, to keep on spooning the burning liqueur over the omelette until the fire has died out.

And a final word: I hope no one will dream of serving these sweet omelettes as an entree, to be eaten with a salad or anything else, as I have known some people to suggest in my restaurant. They are dessert omelettes.

Someone once asked me, "Madame, what is your most exotic omelette?" That would be hard to say. Some might think the one with rooster combs that I have already given would qualify. But there is a specialty of Lyon that is most unusual, and I give it here, to close my selection of recipes, for the benefit of those who live in California or any of the few other parts of the United States where the acacia tree blooms.

OMELETTE AUX FLEURS D'ACACIA Make the OME-LETTE SUCREE. Chop some acacia flowers and put them in the center of the omelette. Sprinkle with sugar. When the omelette is folded, add 2 or 3 tablespoons of kirsch.

CHAPTER 4

The Salad

A lady who had eaten her salad in my restaurant one day paid me a wry compliment, in which there may have been some envy as well as appreciation. "These leaves are so well inpregnated with the dressing," she exclaimed. "Do you put the dressing on every leaf with a brush?"

"How many customers do you think I could serve if I did that?" I asked her, smiling.

Other customers ask me how I make my dressing, and inquire why I don't sell it. They tell me it is the best they ever tasted. In answer to the last question, I have never tried to sell it because I can do no more in my small kitchen than I am doing now, and I have no time or space to make any more than I can use. Perhaps one day I shall sell it.

As for how it is made, I shall tell you forthwith. The first principle is that the leaves must be absolutely dry. Almost the first thing I do when I come to work in the morning is to dry each leaf with a towel. Of course it is a tedious job.

If that method is too slow for you, perhaps you will find another way to do the drying, but dry it must be.

When you are making a salad, prepare the leaves in advance and keep them in a cellophane bag in your refrigerator, or in a large container with a cover. They can even be prepared the day before. But remember, if they are not dry, no amount of dressing will prevent them from being without taste, or at best with a watery taste. If a salad is dried properly, only a small amount of dressing will be needed. Taste first, and if you think there is not enough, add a little more.

One day I had a customer who begged me to sell him a little jar of dressing, and when he asked me how much he should use, I told him that for an individual salad like mine, one tablespoonful should be enough, and I advised him to have his salad dry. He came back the next day and accused me of not selling him my dressing because, he said, his salad had no taste. I told him I had no other dressing in the kitchen than mine. A little more conversation, and the mystery was solved. He had made a large salad, because it was to feed his wife and children as well, and he had put only one tablespoon of dressing on it, the amount needed for the individual salad he had eaten in my restaurant. No wonder it had no taste!

"Couldn't you taste it, and add more dressing when you saw it was tasteless?" I asked him.

"No," he insisted, but now a little sheepishly. "You told us one tablespoon, and that's what we used."

Please remember, then, to taste before you eat. The measures I am going to give you are for *one* salad, and even then it is up to your own taste. Some people like a great deal of dressing on a salad, others do not.

This is how I make my dressing. Use 3 tablespoons of oil to 1 of vinegar, with salt and pepper to taste. Add some mustard and any herbs you like. A French dressing is usually made with dry mustard, but I do not use it, and that is probably what accounts for the different taste. I use prepared mustard, and for the amount noted above, only ¼ teaspoon. If you like mustard particularly and want to put in ½ teaspoon, then use 4 tablespoons of oil, retaining the proportion of vinegar since the mustard takes the place of vinegar. I use a good blended oil and a wine vinegar.

Of course you can use the oil of your choice. Some people think that if they don't use the same oil I use it won't be the same. It is true that if you use olive oil the salad will have a slightly different taste, but that does not mean you will not have a good dressing. As with all cookery, you must experiment.

I advise you to make a jar of dressing. It keeps well for a great length of time without being put in the refrigerator. If you want to keep it longer, put it in the bottom of the refrigerator in the summer months. In the winter refrigeration is not necessary. If you keep it outside, however, be sure it is not in too warm a place. The danger of keeping it in the refrigerator is that it will become too thick if it is near the ice or the freezing unit. To make a jar, put in about 2 cups of oil, ¾ of a cup of wine vinegar, 3 tablespoons of prepared mustard, 2 level tablespoons of salt, and ¾ tablespoon of pepper. Mix well.

Pay no attention to anyone who says you should put sugar in a dressing. I have never seen a French dressing with sugar, and I hope I never have the misfortune to taste one.

If you want to do a vegetable salad, increase the proportions of salt and pepper, as well as those of vinegar and mustard.

In the matter of buying lettuce, it is strange that everyone likes a white salad, because the vitamins are in the green.

White lettuce is made by tying the lettuce so that it never sees the sun, which of course makes it tender. But the green leaves exposed to the sun are the ones with vitamins. People go out in the sun to be healthy, and lie exposed to it until they are brown. It is the same thing with the lettuce that goes into your salad. The lettuce does not get brown in the sun, but becomes a very dark green. It is not as tender, but it is much healthier. I eat only the green, but because it is tougher, I cut it very fine.

Gourmets do not all agree about when the salad should be served. Some think it should come first, so that it may be tasted for itself and serve as a course in the meal. Others believe it should be the accompaniment to the entree, and still others think it should be the refreshing divider between entree and dessert. Since there is so much difference in opinion and in taste, is it not wise to serve it at once, so that it may be eaten whenever the diner likes to have it? If it is a good salad it will have its own dignity and its own place in the meal whenever it is eaten.

Now you should have no difficulty in making that good salad.

❧ ❧ ❧ CHAPTER 5

Wine with Omelettes —
and without

There is so much literature about wines, and so much dis-
agreement about them, that perhaps it is presumptuous of
me to pitch in my five francs' worth. But as you must know
from reading this book, I am not a woman who hesitates to
express her opinion, and about good food and wine I have
opinions.

What I will have to say about wines is brief, no more than
a note, really, but let me tell you that I believe wine with
food is almost indispensable. I know that this is the belief
of the French more than any other people, but is not France
the home of gastronomy?

Here in America, I understand, people are gradually beginning to appreciate wine with their meals, but it is still
far from being a part of their way of life, as it is in France. A
carafe of wine on the dinner table, so common in France, is
hardly seen here at all. There seems to be no cheap but good

wine which can be served in this way. One must order a bottle, and if it is good, it is likely to be expensive.

In my restaurant I have no liquor license, and so wine is not served. Even if I had the license there would be no room to keep a cellar, and no time to give it the careful attention a cellar with any pretensions must have. Patrons may bring their wine with them, and many do. They are usually the ones who have traveled and have learned what a joy and comfort it is to have a good wine with a meal.

But Americans, so I understand, are drinking wine at home more and more, and it is to encourage this excellent trend that I will tell you here what I consider the best wines for the various kinds of food. They are what I would call wines of harmony, since I do not believe that simple correctness is enough. A wine may be correct without being particularly harmonious.

With an omelette or any egg dish, a rosé or white wine is best. This may be a white Bandol or other Côte de Provence (white or rosé), a white Côtes du Rhône, or rosé such as Tavel or Lirac.

With hors d'oeuvre, a white wine from the Marne may be served, or a Meursault, or a Pouilly, or chablis. Ordinarily, I suppose, one does not serve wine with hors d'oeuvre except on very special gastronomic occasions, but there is no law that says you must not if you have the inclination, and like any other food, hors d'oeuvre are enhanced by such wines.

With pâtés, ham, or salmis, one may serve Beaujolais, or Bordeaux (St. Estèphe or St. Julien), a Loire, or a Muscadet. When you are serving *foie gras*, however, a light champagne is better.

With fish there is a wide choice, but the general rule is that it must be a white wine, a Burgundy such as Meursault, Corton blanc, Puligny-Montrachet—Côtes du Rhône, or Alsace

Riesling. All the Bordeaux white wines (even sauternes) are acceptable, and so is champagne *brut*.

For oysters and all similar seafoods, including coquilles, I recommend a Pouilly or chablis, Muscadet, and the dry Bordeaux white wines from the Graves district such as Château Carbonnieux—also champagne *brut*.

For lobster, or the tenderer langouste, which is common to the Continent but must be imported here, there is Château Yquem, and white Bordeaux from the châteaux of Guiraud and Rabaud, and also sparkling Vouvray.

With such entrees as sausages and tongue, the Beaujolais wines are best. You will forgive me if I am a little sentimental about these wines, because they come from my portion of France, southern Burgundy, and are particularly beloved in Lyon, of which Guignol said, "Three rivers bathe Lyon: the Rhône, the Saône, and the Beaujolais." These Beaujolais wines should, in general, be drunk when they are young, and always at room temperature. The ones I recommend here are those from Fleurie, which are more fruity; the wine of Juliénas, often considered the best; and the heavier Moulin-à-Vent, perhaps the best available in America. Bordeaux red wines are also good with these entrees, such as the wines of St. Estèphe, and of Château Lafite.

When it comes to roasts and *grillades*, the list is extensive: the Beaujolais wines again, particularly those of Juliénas and Moulin-à-Vent; the red Bordeaux wines, especially St. Emilion, St. Estèphe and St. Julien, as well as other Médoc growths; and the red Burgundy wines, Volnay, Pommard, Nuits-St.-Georges, and again champagne *brut*.

The Beaujolais wines are excellent when served with cheeses such as pont l'évêque and port salut. With brie, camembert, roquefort and bleu, Burgundies such as Corton, Pommard, and the wines of the Côtes du Rhône are better.

For desserts such as fruits, there is champagne *brut*, of course, really a most useful wine; and for sweets there is champagne *demi-sec*. Ice cream, in any of its forms, asks for champagne *sec*, Château Yquem, or any of the sauternes.

These are my preferences. Perhaps you may have your own. There are gourmets who believe that most of the literature about wine is so much chi-chi, and that a good white wine may be taken with anything. That, too, is a preference. Whatever yours may be, the important thing is to have a wine. It is the necessary and perfect complement to fine food.

CHAPTER 6

Some Notes on Omelette Eaters

Someone has written that a restaurant is the best school in the world to learn about human nature. This is a truth to which I can attest. I have been learning since I was twelve, and I am still learning. It has been my good fortune to entertain in my place some of the noted people in the world, and I have found nearly all of them charming and considerate. Many have become my friends. The good things these people have said about me in their travels are responsible for spreading the fame of my little restaurant around the world.

I do not mean that my patrons who are not celebrities are any less charming and considerate. But because there are more of them, I suppose, it happens sometimes that I encounter those who drive me out of my mind with gastronomic barbarities or impossible demands. This has been good for my character, I think. I have a temper certainly no longer than the average, but I have learned to treat these people with dignity and restraint, and to do what I can for them without letting my indignation spill over.

One of the earliest incidents I remember which compelled me to take a tight rein on my Gallic temper concerns the lady who looked for a long time at my menu, listing omelettes with ham, cheese, mushrooms, tomatoes, *fines herbes,* and other things, then handed it back to me. "I don't want that," she said, in a tone as cold as the bitter north wind which blows down the Rhône. "I want an omelette made with eggs."

What, I ask you, is one to say to that?

However, one lesson I have learned is that where eating is concerned you can lead people only up to a point. It is reasonable to think that from a menu listing more than five hundred different kinds of omelettes, it would be possible for most people to find something to their liking. You may imagine, then, why I always feel a little shaken when a patron glances vaguely at my menu, leans back, and says blankly, "I don't know what I want. I like anything, really. What do you recommend, madame?"

Naturally I recommend every omelette appearing on my menu. If I did not, I would not be making them. Unless I have served a customer regularly for some time, I can hardly know what he likes and will therefore want. Fortunately I had a thorough training by my parents in dealing not only with cuisine but with the unpredictabilities of the public, and so I have learned to expect that a certain percentage of patrons simply do not possess the temperament to deal with the problem of deciding.

My waitress, Yvonne, has been with me for a long time— she is my friend and helper in many ways, along with her regular duties. Like me, she is French and does not care greatly for insouciance when it comes to ordering. "No," I hear her saying with firmness, "I cannot go to the kitchen and say to Madame, 'The patron says he likes ham, but you can give him anything.'"

There is a risk in choosing for people. For example, one day five customers came in together, saying they had been sent by friends. Four of them chose omelettes, but the other one said to me, "I'm a steak man myself. I come from Texas."

"Then why did you come here, monsieur," I asked him, "where only omelettes are served?"

"Okay," he said, with a big Texas laugh, "then make me something wonderful in the omelette line."

Thinking this something of a challenge, I made him one of my best omelettes, the Edouard Herriot, which is with *foie gras*, truffles, chicken, and *sauce cognac*. When he came to pay the bill I said, "Well, monsieur, how did you like it?"

"I'm still a steak man," he said genially.

As such a man really has no need of my place, I could only say, restraining my temper, "Monsieur, I am sure you will be better served somewhere else another time."

Sometimes, when I have had a particularly hard day, I still have a small nightmare about a lady who arrived with her husband and her dog, prepared to be served lunch. One might almost say she dared us to serve her lunch.

"I have been told you know how to make an omelette," she said. "Do you?"

"I think so, madame," I said.

"I like an omelette very well done," she went on. "That is the only way I will eat it."

With pain, for that is not the correct way to cook an omelette, I cooked it a little more than usual. But when it was served to her, she sent it back. "It is not cooked enough," Yvonne reported, looking more upset than I was. "She says you must cook it more." I made another, cooked even more. Back it came again. I felt it was time for me to speak.

"Madame," I said, "this is not an omelette, it is a pancake, and I do not specialize in the pancake."

As I spoke the lady was giving a piece of the omelette to her dog, an ancient and dyspeptic animal, who turned his head away.

"There, you see?" my patron cried triumphantly. "Even the *dog* knows this is not cooked properly."

I restrained myself from putting the rest of the omelette in her face and only remarked, "Yes, madame, your dog knows it is cooked too much."

Next day the husband returned, alone and in visible discomfort, to apologize. "My wife is rather a nervous woman," he explained, sighing. I could not have agreed with him more, and only hoped that the *omelette aux champignons* I had given him provided a period of pleasant forgetfulness, however brief.

The gastronomic eccentricities of some people are quite beyond belief. I cannot believe that I really experienced one incident which ranks foremost in my chamber of horrors; certainly I hope I shall not live to see it repeated.

A gentleman came into my restaurant alone one day, and it was to be seen at once that he was in a state of eager anticipation.

"What omelette will be to your taste today, monsieur?" I asked him.

"Ah, madame," he said with pleasure, "I want an *omelette au rhum*. But first—" He paused. It was about three o'clock in the afternoon and I was alone; I supposed he was thinking such an omelette would take a long time to prepare.

"First, monsieur?"

"Yes, first I will have a *salade* with garlic."

I tried to compose my nerves and speak, but I could not for a moment. It was truly frightening—a salad with garlic, to be followed by a rum omelette. What a disaster for the stomach! My patron seemed otherwise to be a charming man, and I would certainly lose him as a customer. People remember with hostility a restaurant where they ate something which drove them in the middle of the night to the medicine cabinet.

"But, monsieur," I said, remonstrating, "you don't mean to eat a rum omelette on top of garlic, I hope?"

"And why not?" he inquired gaily. "After all, madame, I am the one who is eating it."

That was true. I gave him the salad, and when he had finished it, he called for another one, this time to be made with onions. I thought he would say then, "Never mind the *omelette au rhum*, madame," but he was obviously waiting for it, so I made it.

When he was finished, I said: "Monsieur, if you had struck me, you could not have hurt me more. This has been an insult to French cooking."

He only rubbed his stomach cheerfully. "Well, it was good *here*, madame," he assured me.

But I never saw him again. If I had known his name I would have looked for it in the death notices in the newspaper.

These are extremes, of course, but there are much more familiar American habits of eating to which I cannot accustom myself. In France, diners respect desires other than hunger which bring them to the table. For example, there is the desire to taste each item, as itself and at its best. In America it is common for people to eat several things at once, in hysterical combination, losing the taste of each. Sometimes it appears that taste is an enemy. The true *cuisinière* knows that the appropriate destiny for a fine sauce is to bestow a light caress on a dish. Too many people regard a sauce as something to hurl on food, smothering what well may be a questionable alliance of fish and poultry, or meat and vegetables.

The drinking of water with every other mouthful is also a puzzlement to the French, and not only because the custom of the country is wine, not water, with meals. Wine companions food; water drowns what is being eaten. I have often wondered if the reason for so much bitter complaint here about heartburn and stomach trouble is not due to this obstinate drowning of meals with water, and too much ice.

But enough of complaints and barbaric customers! You will not believe I have had any interesting or satisfying patrons, and I have had thousands of them.

I think Grace Moore must have been the first celebrity in my Salon de Thé soon after it opened; at least she was the first one known to me, although at first I did not recognize her. She came in one day, beautiful and vivacious, and said to me, "I find myself giving a sudden party and I need three dozen petits fours. Do you have them?"

I wasn't sure and feared I might lose the sale, but we counted together with care, and there were two dozen and ten. "Bravo, madame!" she cried. "I am saved. I will never forget you. In fact, I will come back in a few days for more."

Not only did Miss Moore come back, but she returned often as long as she lived, and became my friend. She had a great fondness for an omelette with chocolate sauce, which made her friends cry out in horror when she ordered it. But ask yourself why this should seem so bizarre? Are not eggs combined with chocolate in mousse, and chocolate cream pie? Of course. Why, then, should eggs not combine with chocolate sauce for an omelette?

Friends told friends about my place and celebrities told

celebrities. It may have been Miss Moore who inspired her colleague at the Metropolitan Opera, Lily Pons, to come. I had never seen her before, but her name stirred in me a memory of long ago. Then I remembered—Lyon, about 1916. She was only twelve years old then, singing in one of the cafés in our town. Everybody was saying, "You must go to hear the young girl with the beautiful voice." Everyone was predicting she would be famous some day, and so she was. I wanted to hear her sing so much, but I was working very hard and had not the time to go several kilometers into the city. And now here she was, a reigning star at the Metropolitan, coming into my Salon de Thé for pastries and coffee in the afternoons.

My brief experience at the Blue Angel resulted in my acquiring another regular customer, not yet a great star but on his way. Mr. Jacoby had introduced to me a young man who was performing there, singing to his own guitar accompaniment. He wore a costume of tight black pants and a black silk shirt, and appeared to be fluent in at least seven or eight languages. To my ear his French was beautiful. His name was Yul Brynner, and he came often to my place with his fiancée, Miss Virginia Gilmore. After they were married, they came to be regular visitors.

In those early days at 137½, it seemed to me that the celebrities who came were attracted by dishes they could not get elsewhere. For instance, the noted conductor, Leopold Stokowski, was one of the first to discover that he could get me to make a dessert omelette. The maestro was always coming in for one of my small round layer cakes, made with a cream filling, and covered over with the *chocolat*. One day he overheard someone speak of my omelettes, although I did not yet have a menu of them. I made them sometimes by request.

"If I come sometime when I am not very hungry and would like something light and delicious," Maestro Stokowski said, "would you make me an omelette with apricots? I am very fond of apricots."

In a somewhat similar way, Marlene Dietrich came to me for the potato omelettes she liked so much. When anyone tells me they adore potato omelettes but they are much too fattening, I only point out Miss Dietrich, certainly the most svelte grandmother extant.

I did not realize how well known my omelettes had become until I heard one day the flattering story that Madame Pandit had told someone in New Delhi that one of the first things she meant to do in America when she came to the United Nations was to visit me and have an omelette, which she did.

Such publicity can only come from the kind things these famous people say to each other about me, in that fraternity of celebrity which stretches around the world into all the great capitals. Many of these people have been good enough to give me autographed pictures which today nearly cover the walls of my restaurant. It is an impressive array: Maurice Chevalier, Charles Boyer, Melvyn Douglas, Fernandel, Helen Jepson and Rose Bampton (those two were photographed with me inside my place), Sylvia Marlowe, Denise Darcel, Beulah Bondi, Virginia Gilmore, Robert Trout, Judy Holliday, Julie Harris, Richard Barthelmess, Renee Jeanmaire, Colette Marchand, Bonita Granville, Adele Astaire, Tyrone Power, Rock Hudson, Tony Perkins, Montgomery Clift, Joan McCracken, Vernon Duke, Geraldine Fitzgerald, Larry McPhail, Lady Mendl (I have a letter from her thanking me for a wonderful dinner), Greta Garbo, Charles Laughton, and Elsa Lanchester, the Lowell Thomases, Bennett Cerf, Yehudi Menuhin, Gloria Vanderbilt, Paul Gallico, Mrs. DeWitt Wallace, Elsa Maxwell, Katharine Cornell, Sally Ann Howes, Jean Sablon, Charles Trenet, and many others.

These are some of the noted people who look down from my walls on the little area of nine tables where once they ate my omelettes. Many still come as their careers bring them to New York. Some, it is sad to say, have died. But every day new faces appear, some of them familiar to me from their pictures in the newspapers, and others like the young Don Loper, people who will one day be known to everyone. One of my most special customers is a very nice lawyer who gave me much good professional advice when I first started, and today is my very good friend. His name is Robert B. Healey.

Naturally I am flattered to entertain such people and pleased that they think so well of my cooking. But I would not have you believe that my restaurant is a glittering meeting place for celebrities from the worlds of music, theater, ballet, society and politics, although on occasion, I am happy to tell you, it has looked that way. It is really a small and unpretentious room occupied and often filled to overflowing with people like yourselves who have come there, as do the celebrities, not to see and be seen, which is the case in some well known places, but simply to eat fine food—omelettes and salads, with brioche and a French pastry to finish.

I will always be glad to see you at 32 East 61st Street, New York, New York, but I hope that this book of mine will be an inspiration to you to re-create the good food I serve in your own home. It will take your patience and perseverance at first, but the result will be worth it. *Bon appétit!*

Index

Acacias omelette, 82
Aiglon omelette, 81
Aix les Bains omelette, 83
Alexandre Dumas omelette,
    109–10
Algérienne omelette, 69
Ambassadeur omelette, 84
Ampère omelette, 129
Andalouse omelette, 70
Antiboise omelette, 69
Apple omelette, 60–61
Arc de Triomphe omelette,
    127–28
Argenteuil omelette, 63
Arlégeoise omelette, 63
Arlequin omelette, 137
Arlésienne omelette, 68
Armenonville omelette, 107
Artichoke hearts omelette, 54–
    55
Asparagus omelette, 56–57
Aubervilliers omelette, 94
Aurillac omelette, 65–66
Austerlitz omelette, 93
Auteuil omelette, 94
Avignon omelette, 69

Bacon omelettes, 57, 75–78

Bagatelle omelette, 103
Balzac omelette, 102
Bamboche omelette, 65
Bandol omelette, 90
Barbes omelette, 107
Barigoule omelette, 77
Basic sauces:
    blond, 132–33
    poulet au vin, 130–31
Basque omelette, 69–70
Bastille omelette, 101
Bataclan omelette, 107
Batignoles omelette, 94
Baudelaire omelette, 93
Baudette omelette, 81
Bayonnaise omelette, 96
Béarnaise omelette, 96
Beaucaire omelette, 125
Beauharnais omelette, 84
Beauvais omelette, 111
Beauvillier omelette, 64
Béchamel sauce, 134
Beef omelettes, 109–12
Bercy omelette, 92
Biarritz omelette, 97
Bizet omelette, 96–97
Blond sauce, 132–33
Bobino omelette, 127

Boileau omelette, 86
Bois de Boulogne omelette, 105
Bonaparte omelette, 90
Bonne Femme omelette, 95
Bordelaise sauce, 132, 133
Bougival omelette, 86
Boulangère omelette, 77
Boulogne omelette, 70
Bourguignonne sauce, 134
Bovary omelette, 80
Bressane omelette, 64
Bretonne omelette, 88
Brillat Savarin omelette, 103
Brown sauce, 133–34
Bucheronne omelette, 88
Buttes-Chaumont omelette, 78

Café de la Paix omelette, 108
Calf's-brain omelettes, 59–60, 116–18
Calf's-liver omelettes, 122–23
Caprice d'Amour omelette, 138
Capucine omelette, 106
Carillon omelette, 91
Carnot omelette, 73
Carrousel omelette, 108
Cauliflower omelette, 57
Caulincourt omelette, 108
Caumartin omelette, 94
Caviar omelettes, 60, 125–26
Célestins omelette, 87
Cézanne omelette, 125
Chaillot omelette, 94
Chambery omelette, 62
Champagne sauce, 132
Champ de Mars omelette, 93
Champenoise omelette, 65
Champeret omelette, 120
Champs Elysées omelette, 106

Charbonnière omelette, 68
Charentaise omelette, 91
Charollaise omelette, 122
Chasseur omelette, 79
Chasseur sauce, 132
Chateaubriand omelette, 111
Chateaubriand sauce, 134
Château d'If omelette, 111–12
Châteauneuf omelette, 109
Chatelet omelette, 93
Chatillon omelette, 68
Cheese omelettes, 52, 62–66
Chenonceaux omelette, 77
Cherubin omelette, 136
Chestnut omelette, 60
Chicken-liver omelettes, 58–59, 79–82
Chicken omelettes, 58, 99–108
Chimay omelette, 116
Chinon omelette, 123
Chive omelette, 55
Chocolate sauce, 137
Choisy omelette, 63
Chopin omelette, 97
Ciro's omelette, 108
Clamart omelette, 72
Clermont omelette, 110
Clichy omelette, 97
Clos des Lilas omelette, 108
Cluny omelette, 77
Colbert omelette, 72
Colette omelette, 73
Colmar omelette, 66
Concorde omelette, 94
Condorcet omelette, 117
Coq Hardi omelette, 127
Cordeliers omelette, 74
Corneille omelette, 114
Côte d'Azur omelette, 96

Cours Eugénie omelette, 86
Cours Verdun omelette, 70
Courvoisier sauce, 131
Cream sauce, 133
Crécy omelette, 71
Créole omelette, 67
Crillon omelette, 81
Croutons, 112
Cyrano omelette, 80

Danton omelette, 112
D'Arsonval omelette, 124
D'Aubigny omelette, 121
Daudet omelette, 110
Dauphin omelette, 65
Dauphinoise omelette, 63
Deauville omelette, 90
De Balzac omelette, 113
Debussy omelette, 97
De Castellane omelette, 86
Delicieuse omelette, 136
De Lignières omelette, 93
Denise omelette, 125
Desaugiers omelette, 99
Desmoulins omelette, 110–11
De Valvert omelette, 86
De Vigny omelette, 89
Dinard omelette, 89
Directoire omelette, 106
Duhamel omelette, 114
Dumonteil omelette, 65

Eden Roc omelette, 91
Edouard Herriot omelette, 106
Eggplant omelette, 56
Eldorado omelette, 101–2
Emile Zola omelette, 100
Epernay omelette, 94
Epinay omelette, 126

Fantaisie glaciale omelette, 139
Fantasio omelette, 66
Faubonne omelette, 77
Fernandel omelette, 98
Ferrandière omelette, 117
Feu follet omelette, 136
Feuillat omelette, 125
Feydeau omelette, 89
Fidelio omelette, 107
Figeac omelette, 97
Filled omelette, cooking, 47–48
Financière omelette, 79–80
Fines herbes sauce, 133
Flamande omelette, 97
Flammarion omelette, 128
Flaubert omelette, 100
Fleurieu omelette, 78
Florent omelette, 88
Florentine omelette, 72
Foie gras omelettes, 127–28
Fontainebleau omelette, 63–64
Forestière omelette, 89
Fouquet omelette, 89
Franche-Comtoise omelette, 65
François Coppée omelette, 93
Fréjus omelette, 78
French bacon omelettes. *See* Bacon omelettes

Garlic omelette, 55
Gasconne omelette, 95
Gauloise omelette, 71
George Sand omelette, 81
Gérard Philippe omelette, 85
Gerardmer omelette, 111
Giraudoux omelette, 121
Gobelins omelette, 123
Goose-liver omelette, 59
Grand Armagnac sauce, 131

Grand Duc omelette, 96
Grand'mère omelette, 75
Grand Vatel omelette, 81
Grilled chicken omelettes, 99–108
Guignol omelette, 62

Ham omelettes, 58, 95–98
Henri IV omelette, 101
Herbouville omelette, 129
Hermitage omelette, 115
Heyrieux omelette, 78
Honfleur omelette, 73

Impériale omelette, 84

Jacobin omelette, 114
Jacquard omelette, 121
Jacquemard omelette, 114
Jardinière omelette, 70–71
Jean Bart omelette, 118
Jean Cocteau omelette, 98
Jean de Tournès omelette, 86
Jean Jacques Rousseau omelette, 93
Jean Mace omelette, 118
Jean Vallier omelette, 87
Jerusalem artichoke omelette, 54
Joconde omelette, 128
Joinville omelette, 69
Jourdan omelette, 126
Juan les Pins omelette, 90
Jules Romain omelette, 93
Jules Verne omelette, 89
Juliénas omelette, 97
Jusserand omelette, 126
Jussieu omelette, 123

Kidney omelette, 58. *See also* Veal-kidney omelettes, 83

La Cascade omelette, 108
La Colisée omelette, 81
La Coupole omelette, 105
Lafayette omelette, 74
La Feuillée omelette, 74
La Fontaine omelette, 102–3
Lamartine omelette, 113
Lamballe omelette, 77
Lamothe omelette, 121
Langeais omelette, 77
Lapérouse omelette, 81
Lard, 75
Lardons, 75
La Roseraie omelette, 106
La Rotonde omelette, 108
Laurentienne omelette, 62
Lavoisier omelette, 81
Le Colombier omelette, 108
Le Doyen omelette, 101
Le Touquet omelette, 90
Le Vesinet omelette, 74
Lido omelette, 106
Lily Pons omelette, 79
Limousine omelette, 64
Lobster omelettes, 124–25
Longchamps omelette, 94
Lorraine omelette, 64
Louis XIV omelette, 103
Louis Jouvet omelette, 97
Lucullus omelette, 127
Luxembourg omelette, 103
Lyonnaise omelette, 53
Lyonnaise sauce, 133

Maconnaise omelette, 122

Madame de Sévigné omelette, 81

Madeira sauce, 131

Madelon omelette, 72

Maintenon omelette, 102

Maison omelette, 79

Malmaison omelette, 101

Manon omelette, 76

Marbeuf omelette, 93

Marceau omelette, 84–85

Maréchale omelette, 84

Marengo omelette, 88

Margot omelette, 66

Maria omelette, 62–63

Marianne omelette, 68

Marie Stuart omelette, 81

Marignan omelette, 77

Marquise omelette, 136–37

Massena omelette, 77

Massenet omelette, 76

Matignon omelette, 69

Maxim's omelette, 112

Mayol omelette, 98

Mazarin omelette, 93

Médici omelette, 80

Medrano omelette, 107

Menton omelette, 115

Mephisto omelette, 138–39

Mère Brazier omelette, 104

Mère Filloux omelette, 104

Merveilleuse omelette, 119–20

Métropole omelette, 111

Michelet omelette, 125

Michodière omelette, 108

Mignon omelette, 96

Mirabeau omelette, 125

Mireille omelette, 67

Mistral omelette, 68

Mixed herbs omelette, 55–56

Moissonneur omelette, 73

Molière omelette, 110

Monaco omelette, 95–96

Mona Lisa omelette, 101

Monegasque omelette, 70

Monselet omelette, 76

Montagne omelette, 99–100

Montargis omelette, 72

Montbrison omelette, 69

Monte Carlo omelette, 96

Monte Cristo omelette, 89

Montparnasse omelette, 98

Montpellier omelette, 66

Montpensier omelette, 97

Montreuil omelette, 70

Montserrat omelette, 97

Morlaix omelette, 115

Mornay omelette, 64

Mozart omelette, 97

Mulatière omelette, 74

Murat omelette, 97

Mushroom omelettes, 56, 88–91

Napoléon omelette, 85

Neufchâtel omelette, 68

Neuilly omelette, 89

Neuville omelette, 124

Niçoise omelette, 67

Nimoise omelette, 67

Nogent omelette, 89

Normande omelette, 137

Normandie omelette, 93

Odéon omelette, 105–6

Olympia omelette, 128

Omelettes:
    à l'ail (garlic), 55
    aux asperges (asparagus), 56–57

Omelettes (cont'd)
à l'aubergine (eggplant), 56
Bar-le-duc (currant jelly), 135-36
au boeuf (beef), 109-12
au caviar (caviar), 60, 125-26
à la cervelle (calf's-brain), 59-60, 116-18
aux champignons (mushroom), 56, 88-91
au chou-fleur (cauliflower), 57
à la ciboulette (chive), 55
classifications, 50
aux coeurs d'artichaux (artichoke hearts), 54-55
cooking, 44 ff
aux croûtons (toasted bread), 53
à l'épinard (spinach), 56
aux fines herbes (mixed herbs), 55-56
aux foies de poulet (chicken-liver), 58-59, 79-82
au foie de veau (calf's-liver), 122-23
au foie gras (goose-liver), 59, 127-28
au fromage (cheese), 52, 62-66
au homard (lobster), 124-25
au jambon (ham), 58, 95-98
au lard (bacon), 57, 75-78
Lyonnaise, 53
aux marrons (chestnut), 60
aux noix (walnut), 60
à l'oignon (onion), 53
à l'oseille (sorrel or sour-grass), 57

pan, 41-43
aux pommes (apple), 60-61
aux pommes de terre (potato), 53
au poulet (chicken), 58
au poulet grillé (grilled or roast chicken), 99-108
Le Progrès de Lyon, 128
au riz de veau (sweetbread), 60, 119-21
aux rognons de veau (veal kidney), 83-87
aux salsifis (oyster plant), 53-54
aux saucisses (sausage), 58, 92-94
sucrée (sweet), 135-39
aux tomates (tomato), 52, 67-74
aux topinambours (Jerusalem artichoke), 54
aux truffes (truffle), 59
au veau (veal), 113-15
wines with, 145
Onion omelette, 53
Opera omelette, 137
Orée du Bois omelette, 106
Orléans omelette, 77
Orly omelette, 127
Ornano omelette, 107
Oyster plant omelette, 53-54
Oyster sauce, 133

Palais Grillet omelette, 87
Palais Rameau omelette, 87
Palais Royal omelette, 127
Pam Pam omelette, 107
Parc Monceau omelette, 107
Parisienne omelette, 92

Parmentier omelette, 62
Pascal omelette, 123
Passy omelette, 93
Paysanne omelette, 75
Pergola omelette, 107
Perigord omelette, 128
Perpignan omelette, 90
Petite Fermière omelette, 95
Pierre Dupont omelette, 100
Pigalle omelette, 94
Piperade. *See* Basque omelette
Place Bellecour omelette, 97
Place Carnot omelette, 78
Place du Tertre omelette, 94
Place le Viste omelette, 86
Plain omelette, 46-47
    sweet, 135
Plaza Athénée omelette, 105
Pompadour omelette, 138
Poncet omelette, 75
Pontarlier omelette, 109
Pont Neuf omelette, 73
Pontoise omelette, 115
Pont Tilsitt omelette, 85
Porte Dauphine omelette, 81
Porte Maillot omelette, 93
Porte St. Martin omelette, 97
Potato omelette, 53
Poulbot omelette, 77
Prado omelette, 81
Prince de Sagan omelette, 100-1
Princesse omelette, 79
Provençale omelette, 68
Provence omelette, 117
Prunier omelette, 82

Racine omelette, 114
Raimu omelette, 121

Rambouillet omelette, 108
Ramponeau omelette, 121
Raynouard omelette, 126
Réaumur omelette, 120
Récamier omelette, 80
Régence omelette, 80
Réjane omelette, 80
Renaissance omelette, 102
Rêve doré omelette, 137
Richelieu omelette, 100
Riviera omelette, 90
Rivoli omelette, 87
Roast chicken omelettes, 99-108
Robinson omelette, 122
Rochambeau omelette, 65
Rochechouart omelette, 94
Rohans omelette, 81
Rond Point omelette, 107
Ronsard omelette, 123
Rostand omelette, 102
Roubaix omelette, 123
Rouget de Lisle omelette, 116-17
Roussillon omelette, 120
Rouville omelette, 117
Roxane omelette, 81
Royale sauce, 132
Royal Haussmann omelette, 106
Royal Monceau omelette, 108
Royans omelette, 123
Rum omelette. *See* Feu follet omelette

St. Auber omelette, 73
St. Cloud omelette, 98
St. Denis omelette, 126
St. Maxime omelette, 90
St. Peray omelette, 90

St. Remy omelette, 126
St. Saëns omelette, 100
Salads, 140–43
Salmon omelettes, 126
Sarah Bernhardt omelette, 104
Sauces, 130–33
    basic:
        blond, 132–33
        poulet au vin, 130–31
    béchamel, 134
    blond, 132–33
    bordelaise, 132, 133
    bourguignonne, 134
    brown, 133–34
    champagne, 132
    charcutière, 133–34
    chasseur, 132
    chateaubriand, 134
    chocolate, 137
    Courvoisier, 131
    cream, 133
    fines herbes, 133
    Grand Armagnac, 131
    Lyonnaise, 133
    madeira, 131
    oyster, 133
    royale, 132
    sherry, 131
    supreme, 131
    tomato, 134
    velouté, 134
    white, 134
Saumur omelette, 121
Sausage omelettes, 58, 92–94
Savoyarde omelette, 71
Scaramouche omelette, 117
Sebastopol omelette, 86
Sedan omelette, 87
Ségur omelette, 90

Serignan omelette, 125
Sherry sauce, 131
Solférino omelette, 86
Sorrel omelette, 57
Soubise omelette, 76
Sourgrass omelette, 57
Souveraine omelette, 136
Spinach omelette, 56
Suffren omelette, 113–14
Sully omelette, 114
Sultane omelette, 97
Supreme omelette, 138
Supreme sauce, 131
Sweetbread omelettes, 60, 119–21
Sweet omelettes, 135–39
    arlequin, 137
    Bar-le-duc, 135–36
    caprice d'amour, 138
    cherubin, 136
    delicieuse, 136
    fantaisie glaciale, 139
    feu follet, 136
    aux fleurs d'acacia, 139
    marquise, 136–37
    mephisto, 138–39
    normande, 137
    opera, 137
    plain, 135
    pompadour, 138
    rêve doré, 137
    souveraine, 136
    supreme, 138

Tabarin omelette, 105
Taillevent omelette, 121
Talleyrand omelette, 86
Tarasconne omelette, 94
Tavernier omelette, 85

Thermidor omelette, 124
Thomassin omelette, 117
Tivoli omelette, 126
Toasted bread omelette, 53
Tolozan omelette, 117
Tomato omelettes, 52, 67–74
Tomato sauce, 134
Tosca omelette, 68
Toulon omelette, 90
Toulouse omelette, 94
Tour d'Argent omelette, 105
Tour Eiffel omelette, 104
Tournon omelette, 78
Trevoux omelette, 83–84
Triomphe omelette, 120
Truffle omelette, 59
Tuileries omelette, 90
Tuna-fish omelettes, 126
Turenne omelette, 124

Val d'Isère omelette, 88
Valenciennes omelette, 63
Valery omelette, 120–21
Valfleury omelette, 71

Valmy omelette, 110
Vauban omelette, 126
Vaubecour omelette, 77
Vaucluse omelette, 78
Vaugirard omelette, 91
Veal-kidney omelettes, 83–87
Veal omelettes, 113–15
Velouté sauce, 134
Vendéenne omelette, 92
Versailles omelette, 83
Vernay omelette, 124
Vert Galant omelette, 81
Villageoise omelette, 71–72
Villeroy omelette, 76
Vincennes omelette, 90
Viroflay omelette, 97
Volnay omelette, 76
Voltaire omelette, 76

Walnut omelette, 60
White sauce, 134
Wines, 144–47

Yvonne omelette, 94

CPSIA information can be obtained
at www.ICGtesting.com
Printed in the USA
BVHW040900210722
642601BV00002B/100